Understanding Anxiety in Relationships

A Self-Help Workbook that Identifies the Signs of Anxiety and Teaches You How to Manage, Fight and Overcome it

© Copyright 2019 by Alison Care - All rights reserved.

This book is provided with the sole purpose of providing relevant information on a specific topic for which every reasonable effort has been made to ensure that it is both accurate and reasonable. Nevertheless, by purchasing this book, you consent to the fact that the author, as well as the publisher, are in no way experts on the topics contained herein, regardless of any claims as such that may be made within. As such, any suggestions or recommendations that are made within are done so purely for entertainment value. It is recommended that you always consult a professional prior to undertaking any of the advice or techniques discussed within.

This is a legally binding declaration that is considered both valid and fair by both the Committee of Publishers Association and the American Bar Association and should be considered as legally binding within the United States.

The reproduction, transmission, and duplication of any of the content found herein, including any specific or extended information will be done as an illegal act regardless of the end form the information ultimately takes. This includes copied versions of the work both physical, digital and audio unless express consent of the Publisher is provided beforehand. Any additional rights reserved.

Furthermore, the information that can be found within the pages described forthwith shall be considered both accurate and truthful when it comes to freely available information and general consent. As such, any use, correct or incorrect, of the provided information will render the Publisher free of responsibility as to the actions taken outside of their direct purview. Regardless, there are zero scenarios where the original author or the Publisher can be deemed liable in any fashion for any damages or hardships that may result from any of the information discussed within.

Finally, any of the content found within is ultimately intended for entertainment purposes and should be thought of and acted on as such. Due to its inherently ephemeral nature, nothing discussed within should be taken as an assurance of quality, even when the words and deeds described herein indicated otherwise. Trademarks and copyrights mentioned within are done for informational purposes in line with fair use and should not be seen as an endorsement from the copyright or trademark holder.

ISBN: 9781099978616

Table of Contents

Introduction **7**

Chapter 1: What Is Anxiety? **18**

   A Paradise Lost 22

   Defining Anxiety 30

   The Causes of Anxiety 37

   Differential Diagnosis for Anxiety 39

Chapter 2: Anxiety Disorders **41**

   The Fear Pathway 44

   Review of Anxiety Disorders 49

   Generalized Anxiety Disorder 52

   Panic Disorder 52

   Specific Phobias 53

   Obsessive-compulsive Disorder 57

   Post-traumatic Stress Disorder 58

   Selective Mutism 59

   Separation Anxiety Disorder 60

Situational Anxiety 61

Social Anxiety Disorder or Social Phobia 61

Agoraphobia 62

Chapter 3: Dating Someone with Anxiety 64

Having the Right Approach to Anxiety 68

Do We Live in a Traumatized Society? 76

Communication is Important (Speak face to face, not via text) 80

Learn to Listen 82

Stay Calm 83

Ask Questions to Understand How Your Partner Feels 84

You Do Not Have to Validate Your Partner's Feelings But At Least Try to Relate to Where They Are Coming From 84

Observation Is Key to Really Coming to Understand Your Partner 86

Do Not Make Assumptions about Their Anxiety 86

Communicate Things Clearly to Your Partner 87

Chapter 4: The Role of Attachment in Relationships with Anxious Individuals 88

Types of Attachment 91

Attachment Problems in Anxious Adults 97

How You Can Overcome Attachment Problems in Your Relationship 99

Chapter 5: Treatment for Anxiety 103

Medication Treatment for Anxiety 106

Therapy for Anxiety 109

Natural Treatments and Alternative Medicine 110

Chapter 6: 10 Tips to Help You Support Your Partner through Anxiety............................. 113

Tip 1: Understand that overcoming anxiety is a process (anxiety is not something that someone will snap out of) 114

Tip 2: Be conscious of your own dysfunctional thoughts or preconceived notions....................................... 115

Tip 3: Provide reassurance that things are going to turn out all right... 115

Tip 4: Encourage your partner to get help.............. 116

Tip 5: Be patient as your significant other moves through their condition 117

Tip 6: Provide ongoing education and support to your partner.. 117

Tip 7: Recognize that no one understands your partner's anxiety more than your partner 118

Tip 8: Be available, not overbearing...................... 119

Tip 9: Take your partner's comments seriously 120

Tip 10: Remember that empathy is important 120

Chapter 7: 10 Habits That Can Make Your Partner's Anxiety Worse............................ 122

Habit 1: Setting Unattainable Goals 123

Habit 2: Unhealthy Dietary Habits (like excessive smoking or alcohol consumption) 124

Habit 3: Excessive Use of Social Media................... 125

Habit 4: Depriving Yourself of Sleep 126

Habit 5: Not Getting Enough Exercise 127

Habit 6: Not Being Honest About How You Are Feeling 127

Habit 7: Magnifying A Situation (Blowing Things Out of Proportion) 128

Habit 8: Not Listening 128

Habit 9: Allowing Your Partner to Isolate Themselves 129

Habit 10: Managing Stress Poorly, Both Inside and Outside a Relationship 129

Frequently Asked Questions....................... 131

Conclusion... 147

Introduction

The role that mental health conditions can play in relationships is a subject that is attracting more attention now than ever before. The increased attention that issues of mental health have received is due to a number of factors including a recognition that mental health impacts the lives of a large number of people, and the understanding that mental health concerns can be improved with increased education. Education is important for mental health providers, teachers and other educators, and individuals who are suffering from mental illness. In truth, education about conditions like anxiety may be just as important for the family and friends of people suffering from a disorder as it is for the sufferer.

The reader may be surprised to learn just how common anxiety is. Some believe that anxiety disorders may impact as much as thirty percent of the general population at some point in their life. Men and women around the world will be impacted by anxious symptoms, with millions of people likely to be impacted by anxiety in any given year. It is believed that women are about twice as likely as men to be impacted by anxiety; also, anxiousness is believed to be more common among people in their mid-20s and older which renders anxiety an important area of concern in the working age population. Another surprising statistic about anxiety is that it appears to be more common in Europe and the United States than in other parts of the world.

In reality, anxiety is an umbrella term that includes a number of conditions that can cause people to experience fear or panic. Although these conditions are distinct from one another, many of these conditions are associated with a particular fear pathway in the brain that some scientists regard as characteristic of the human experience of anxiety. This pathway, traveling through a region of the brain known as the amygdala, will be explored in depth in this book, particularly in reference to generalized anxiety disorder and post-traumatic stress disorder. Much research about the stimulation of this pathway has been done in recent years, in particular as it relates to the re-experiencing of trauma in post-traumatic stress disorder (PTSD).

Anxiety that lasts for at least six months and which is not associated with a specific trigger is classified by medical professionals as generalized anxiety disorder. Although laypeople often group different types of worry together with the label of "anxiety," it is important to make distinctions. These distinctions are not only important for medical professionals to understand and treat these conditions, but they have real implications in the lives of impacted individuals. Some psychiatrists believe that specific phobias and social anxiety are actually more common than generalized anxiety. Although different forms of anxiety have commonalities, the treatment recommended by a doctor will differ. For some specific phobias, for example, a doctor may recommend treatment in the form of safe exposure to the phobia trigger until the phobia-afflicted individual becomes desensitized.

One of the goals of *Understanding Anxiety in Relationships: A Self-Help Workbook that Identifies the Signs of Anxiety and Teaches You How to Manage, Fight and Overcome It* is to familiarize the reader with anxiousness as the first step to combating it. Anxiety can have a drastic impact on a relationship and the idea is that the reader will become familiarized enough with anxiousness that they may be able to prevent anxiety from derailing their relationship. It is assumed that the reader is the partner of a person who potentially has an anxious condition. For such people, this book will be useful in identifying the symptoms of anxiety as the first step to fighting it. The book will also be useful for men and women in relationships who may be worried about their own anxious symptoms.

The first chapter goes into detail about what anxiety is and introduces the idea that worry can take different forms. Although some readers may not think of conditions like obsessive-compulsive disorder and post-traumatic stress disorder as anxious in nature, these conditions have traditionally been grouped under the term anxiety disorders and are often treated with the same treatment modalities that are used to treat generalized anxiety. Although anxious disorders will be detailed in a separate chapter, one of the goals of the first chapter is to establish "anxiety" as a distinct experience that is related to the varied conditions that are often referred to as disorders on the anxious spectrum.

A thorough discussion of these anxiety disorders is the goal of the second chapter. Although conditions like PTSD or even specific phobia may seem like potential subjects for different books, many people dealing with anxiousness in their relationships are actually dealing with these conditions that represent a significant proportion of anxiety sufferers worldwide. Although this book is not specifically designed to help the reader combat all of these anxiety disorders, it is important that the reader at least familiarize themselves with them, including the criteria that psychiatrists and other medical professionals use to diagnose them. This will help the reader navigate the process of figuring out what type of anxiety precisely their significant other is afflicted with. This will give the significant other peace of mind as they gain comfort in knowing that the problems facing their relationship have a name.

If you are reading this book, then you likely have an interest in maintaining your relationship even in the face of anxiety. This may seem like a difficult task, but once you understand that anxiousness impacts somewhere between one in four and one in three people in the Western world, then the idea that anxiety can be overcome becomes evident. There are millions of people around the world just like you: people faced with the reality of having to salvage a relationship that has been impacted by generalized anxiety disorder or one of the other disorders explored in this book.

This process of salvaging a relationship requires that the reader have an understanding of just how anxiety can impact a relationship. Understanding how this condition can impact a relationship is very important for the spouses or partners of anxious persons because anxiousness can creep up in ways that people who are not anxious may have difficulty recognizing. Anxious persons may develop a sense of fear or paranoia in situations that do not typically inspire these feelings in people without anxiety. They may become defensive or combative in situations, and this may all be due to the anxiety that they are experiencing. Your compassion as the partner of someone experiencing these sorts of symptoms is important, and this process begins in the third chapter as we begin to understand the role that fear and paranoia can have in relationships.

The question of where anxiety comes from is a layered one. It is a subject as perplexing to the psychological community as it is to the spouses and partners of people dealing with anxiousness. That being said, the role that attachment plays in anxiety is an important one and one that extends beyond mere speculation. Attachment theory explores how the bonds that children form with their caregiver may be healthy or dysfunctional. A dysfunctional attachment can be observed by the psychiatrist and can have a significant impact on the relationships that the individual has later on in life. Understanding this allows the reader to get a sense of the gestalt of anxiety, especially as it relates to the interpersonal relationships of anxious persons.

Anxiety is not a condition that has to impede a relationship for the duration of the relationship. Worry does not have to weigh down the person with anxiousness. Anxiety treatment is an area that has been studied for over a century, and there are many effective treatments for anxiety available. Anxiety may take the form of medication, although it does not have to. Therapy, diet, and lifestyle changes have all been shown to be effective in treating this condition in some people. The various forms that anxiety treatment can take will be explored in the fourth chapter.

There are alternative medical treatments for anxiety, including herbal remedies. This is a topic that has attracted great interest of late as part of a movement away from pharmaceutical prescriptions in order to treat common conditions. Alternative medical treatments, including herbal remedies, have been used to treat anxiety longer than anyone can say. Indeed, the ancients recognized anxiety and depression as conditions that men and women faced and they proposed treatments centuries before drug treatments were understood, at least in the way that we understand them today. The reader will gain an understanding of the holistic remedies that can potentially play a role in anxiety treatment in the relationship context.

A great approach for a spouse or partner to have when it comes to managing anxiety in the relationship context is to have tips or tricks that they use to help them deal with the more difficult interactions that they are likely to have with their partner. No one is expected to be wholly understanding or tolerant all of the time. There will be moments when you will lose patience with your partner's anxiety, just as there are moments when your partner is likely to lose patience with those aspects of your personality they find quirky, trying, or otherwise idiosyncratic.

The sixth chapter is designed to help the partner of an anxious person deal with dysfunctional thoughts, allowing the partner to take on an important supportive role. In this regard, anxiety can be similar to depression. Both depression and anxiety can be associated with a downward spiral of negative or dysfunctional thinking. Depressed or anxious people may have a tendency to catastrophize events: that is, to perceive events impacting them in their life to be much worse than they really are.

A good spouse or partner is able to support their significant other even through their difficult moments. Of course, this all begins with the understanding that is gained by educating yourself about mental health conditions like anxiety. But developing a toolkit for dealing with anxiousness in certain contexts doesn't hurt. In the sixth chapter, the reader will learn the 10 tips that they can use to support their partner through their condition. Although as a spouse or partner you may hope to fix your partner's condition or to steer your partner in such a way that their condition disappears (to fit your needs and expectations), perhaps the best way to approach anxiety in a significant other is as a supporter: someone who is available to lend a hand or an ear.

Anxiety is a slippery slope that can easily go from bad to worse in the blink of an eye. In the seventh chapter, the reader will learn the tips that they can use to keep them from making their partner's anxiety worse. Although this book recognizes that everyone is an individual with individual needs, in reality, a supportive partner may be expected to help their partner through their anxiousness by modifying their own behavior slightly so as to not set their partner off. These tips will all be explored in the seventh chapter as the last set of weapons in your war on anxiety arsenal.

It may come as a surprise to some that a condition as common as anxiety can be so debilitating, but millions of individuals and couples have experienced life-changing events due to this condition. By understanding anxiety, the reader can help their partner manage their condition better as well as help themselves to better support an anxious partner. Some readers may be dealing with anxiousness themselves and may have difficulty in recognizing just how anxiety has impacted their relationship. Reading this book will help you to approach your relationship from a new angle, gaining insight that you perhaps did not have before.

One of the goals of *Understanding Anxiety in Relationships: A Self-Help Workbook that Identifies the Signs of Anxiety and Teaches You How to Manage, Fight and Overcome It* is to help anyone dealing with anxiousness in a relationship setting to recognize and modify those behaviors that represent the sturdy foundation of anxiety. The journey begins in the first chapter with a review of just what anxiety is.

Chapter 1:
What Is Anxiety?

There are specific connotations that many people have when it comes to anxiety. Many people imagine an emotional state characterized by a worried facial expression. This expression may feature a furrowed brow, the anxious person is often pictured pacing, there might be bodily complaints such as upset stomach and headache, and finally, the anxious person might vocalize worry or concern about something specific. This picture that some have about worry is part of the larger canvas of anxiety, but as this emotional state can surface in many unique ways, there can be much more to this condition than the image of a worried individual with the furrowed brow that suggests intense thought or fear.

Indeed, anxiety has been a popular subject for philosophers and scientists for over a century. Part of this fascination with anxiousness may stem from the reality that mental illnesses like anxiety and depression commonly impact the same groups that are likely to expound on the subject. Research has suggested that some mental illnesses (including anxiety) are more common in developed Western nations. Studies on this subject have found that anxiety appears to be more common in the United States and Europe than in other parts of the world.

The question of why anxiety appears to be more common in Westernized nations is an interesting one (and one that will be touched on in this book). In psychology, there is the concept of hierarchy of needs. Man's basic needs for life include food, water, and shelter. Needs that reach beyond these basic needs include desires for fulfillment and self-actualization, which essentially represent the sorts of needs that early man theoretically would have been removed from in their daily struggle for survival. When you are busy searching for food or fighting off predators, your priorities may be extending only a few minutes into the future rather than years or decades.

Early man would have been faced with a daily struggle for survival and would likely have had little time to think about long-term life goals and the emotions that go along with success or failure in these endeavors. As an emotion, anxiety would have been something that early humans would have experienced just as they experienced other emotions like joy, sadness, disappointment, and the like, but the fixation with success or failure that is a characteristic of modern Westernized life would have been something that these early people would have had little time for.

It is an interesting subject to ponder because Western society posits that the advancement associated with the Industrial Revolution and what is now a post-Industrial style of life represent an improvement in conditions vis a vis the sort of lifestyle that humans would have been living previously. Modern man in the West (generally) does not have to rise at the crack of dawn to hunt, fish, or hide from the dangers that come along with living in the daylight hours. Modern man also does not have to deal with the high likelihood of his own death or the death of his loved ones from treatable illnesses or mauling by a dangerous predator like a mammoth or a bear. In short, the daily experiences that characterize the life of the humans of today are entirely different than they would have been 10,000 years ago.

This is not to say that Man is a different creature today than he was then. The issue of who and what Man is a subject that was of great fascination to the philosophers of the 18th and 19th century. Thinkers of the Age of Reason like Voltaire were able to look at the world around them with a new lens. They were coming into contact with groups living in the Americas, Africa, and the Pacific who lived differently than how men and women lived and Europe, and who seemed free of some of the cares that modern Europeans of the time seemed to be facing. Though we may see the world a little differently than some of these philosophers did, getting a glimpse back in time in how the philosophes understood their world does give us some insight into the prevalence of anxiety.

A Paradise Lost

Why does anxiety exist? This is a subject that will be explored in this book, particularly as it involves the known brain pathways that appear to be associated with anxiousness. This is a subject that fortunately has been suitably studied and for which there is much data regarding the brain imaging findings that are associated with the subjective experience of fear that individuals with anxiety disorders face as a part of their conditions.

But the study of why anxiousness exists and how it works is one that predates the scientific data that we have access to in the present age. We touched briefly on the subject of the fascination that philosophers (the so-called philosophes) have had when it comes to the state of modern Western man as contrasted with "primitive man." Although the pejorative term "noble savage" has fallen into disuse, this term was used to describe both a common character in fiction of the 18th and 19th centuries and a sort of person that really existed: the men and women who lived outside the boundaries of Western world and who experienced the world differently from Europeans.

The lifestyle of these people was perceived by Europeans to have some advantages when compared to the lives of people of the West. These men and women generally lived without money (currency in the form of coinage or bills), they were often scantily clad (at least in the eyes of the Western onlookers), they did not live in cities but lived off of the land, and they appeared to be free of the stressed and/or manic mental states that were becoming evident even as early as the 17th and 18th centuries. These harried mental states that are more prevalent now had begun to characterize life in Western countries like Britain, France, Spain, and others even then.

Although people today can recognize some elements of prejudice in how these groups living outside the Western world were perceived, studies today suggest that there is a difference in the prevalence of mental illness in Western countries compared to non-Western undeveloped countries. These non-Western countries were places that were only beginning to have contact with Europeans at the time the idea of a paradise lost or a "noble savage" was being developed.

Although many of the minds of this period who explored the idea of this paradise lost were philosophers like Voltaire and Rousseau, writers also found the subject one of interest. Charles Dickens, notable for his popular 19th-century books, wrote extensively on the subject of the peoples that Europeans considered primitive and whom they tended to romanticize. Like many Europeans of the time, he perceived groups like the Inuit of modern-day Alaska and Western Canada as gentle, happy, amiable, and loving, even though he had no personal contact with them and knew only of them from the writings of other Europeans who had made contact with them in their travels.

Indeed, it would be this superficial understanding of a foreign people that would later cause Dickens to change his assessment of the Inuit, a people who were then commonly called Eskimos although this term is now considered offensive by some today. Without going into too much detail about groups like the Inuit and how they were perceived by Europeans, this idea that Europeans were comparing themselves to other "primitive" people and wondering why Europeans were unhappy, depressed, and anxious while people in these other parts of the world seemed not to be is an important aspect of the anxiety issue. Although anxiety is at its simplest an emotion that anyone can experience, the question of why anxiety is more common in certain individuals or even in certain groups is an important one to ask. Understanding the ins and outs of this subject will help the reader to support a partner who is anxious or even perhaps to better understand themselves if they find that anxiety is playing a role in their own life.

The superficiality by which people like Charles Dickens understood non-Europeans is evidenced by the change of line that Dickens took when he learned new information about the Inuit and their interaction with Europeans. As has been stated already, Dickens's understanding of these distant people came solely from the reports he had received in various books and newspapers and which he took at surface value. Dickens himself made his own interpretation of the knowledge that he received from these sources while also seeming to forget that the information itself was colored with the writer or observer's own perceptions.

Dickens and other Englishmen in the 1850s learned that the bodies of Europeans that had traveled to what is now Alaska had been discovered and that there was evidence of cannibalism. It appeared that the Englishmen had found themselves lost and stranded in a place where there was little food and they were unable to survive without resorting to this drastic means for survival. On the surface, it may seem that this finding would have little impact on this perception of the "simplicity" and "nobility" of the groups living in the Americas, that Europeans at the time would perceive this as merely an unfortunate happening within their own group, but that was not the case.

Men like Dickens were horrified at this discovery and accused the Inuit who had found the remains and provided evidence of it as liars and cheats. Perception of groups like the Inuit changed overnight as groups in Britain took the line that when it came down to a "noble savage" and an Englishman in a question of innate goodness, clearly it was the Englishman who was innately good while the "noble savage" – lauded though he may have been by writers and philosophers for over a century – was really capable of anything. It seemed that the Inuit were meant to represent a model that Europeans might follow in order to resume or regain the innate goodness that they perceived was essentially characteristic of Europeans at the time.

In the 19th century, Europeans and European-Americans seemed torn between perceiving non-Europeans as noble in their freedom from the worries and cares that Europeans had and as caricatures that might highlight the innate superiority of Europeans. This led to a discordant message, particularly in the 19th century. This idea of the innate nobility that came from the more natural and innocent sort of life that "savages" lived in the Americas, parts of Asia, and Africa that characterized much of French writing on the subject began to dissipate as the desire to subjugate or profit from the perceived innocence of these non-European peoples intensified.

Writers like Voltaire and Rousseau wrote of groups like the Indians in North America because they were questioning the life that Europeans were living at the present time and essentially seeking to answer the question of whether Man was an essentially good creature. Although philosophers live Voltaire and others seem to reach the eventual conclusion that Man is not inherently good, they seem still to suggest that there are certain aspects of life in Europe at the time that made Man's quest towards goodness more fraught with difficulty than perhaps it was for men and women living in "primitive" and "savage" areas.

This French tradition of seeking to determine the goodness of Man was continued by writers like Honore de Balzac who noted the role that money and concerns about money seemed to have on the character of Europeans and the direction that European society was taking. In works like *The Girl with The Golden Eyes* and *Pere Goriot*, Balzac notes in the style of the time how an obsession with wealth was turning children against their parents and becoming almost a mania. This idea that individuals outside of Europe may have been living in a "paradise" or may have been more "good," "innocent," or "natural" because they were operating outside an essentially mercantile system that brought out the worst in people seems never to be fully explored by Western European thought because they soon became swept up in colonial endeavors. A recognition that these foreign people who were being conquered seemed not to suffer from anxiety and depression was swept to the wayside as the more pressing concern became how such people could be worked into the already existing (and expanding) European financial-mercantile system.

The question of why certain conditions like anxiety and depression seem to be less common in non-Western countries, therefore, remains one of speculation. Although anxiety, like depression, can be attributed to a disturbance in brain chemistry (one that can potentially be treated with medication), it remains to be seen why a condition with an essentially medical cause can not only be more common in some groups than in others but can be induced by the adoption of the accouterments of Western civilization.

The idea of a "paradise lost" and the "noble savage" continues in the Western mindset today with some arguing that this image of the savage represents a deep prejudice while others perhaps see the role that exploring this idea of the savage has had on the Western philosophical tradition. Even the Ancient Greeks explored the idea of a perfect society (as in

Plato's *Republic*), and it was by comparing themselves to the non-European groups that Europeans encountered in the 17th, 18th, and 19th centuries that Europeans began to understand just how their own societies may have been failing in some respects.

Defining Anxiety

Exploring the idea of a "paradise lost" perfectly sets up the question of defining anxiety because it addresses an aspect of mental illness that is often overlooked: the idea that certain types of mental illness appear to be becoming more common and, in some regards, may represent health emergencies. This has made mental illness an aspect of health that not only must be addressed in developed Western nations, but which must be on the radar in nations moving on the path towards Westernization, which is true of nearly all countries in the world due to the efforts of global organizations like the United Nations, World Trade Organization, and International Monetary Fund.

Anxiety is defined as an emotion marked by the experience of fear or worry. Anxiety is, however, to be distinguished from fear, which most scientists regard as a natural reaction to a perceived threat. Anxiousness, therefore, becomes an unnatural or dysfunctional overreaction to stimuli that should not cause fear or the experience of fear to know stimuli at all. Recall that the image of the anxious person is of the man or woman who appears visibly worried, is pacing, or has other somatic or bodily symptoms of anxiety. The idea with anxiousness is that the symptoms of this emotion are perceived to be exaggerated or unnecessary as opposed to fear, which is perceived as having an inherent purpose in human evolution.

In reality, anxiousness and fear are closely related. Research has shown that anxiety is related to the normal fight or flight response that humans experience. Anxiousness (and the anxiety disorders that stem from it) is characterized by the activation of this fight or flight response in situations where it may be generally agreed that this response is not necessary. The fight or flight response is triggered by an event that is perceived as being inherently harmful or threatening.

The fight or flight response is a normal pathway of the sympathetic nervous system. Indeed, the sympathetic nervous system's primary functions are to regulate the body's natural equilibrium or homeostasis and to trigger the fight or flight response. The sympathetic nervous system is part of the body's autonomic nervous system and therefore, represents actions that take place in the body for the most part unconsciously.

The fight or flight response, like other actions in the body that are mediated by the nervous system, occurs through the action of neurotransmitters. In the case of the fight or flight response, the neurotransmitters of import are epinephrine and norepinephrine, which together fall under the category of catecholamines. These are not, however, the only neurotransmitters that play a role in the stress pathway that is characteristic of anxiety. Other neurotransmitters that appear to play a role include serotonin and dopamine, which is part of the reason why medications that target these neurotransmitters are often effective in treating anxiety as well as depression and other conditions.

Anxiousness is an emotional reaction that men and women experience, but people often are referring to anxiety disorder when they use the term anxiety. There are, in fact, several disorders that psychiatrists characterize as anxiety disorders that are related to the essential subjective expensive of anxiety. In truth, anxiousness is not really subjective as there are pathways that have been found to be associated with the experience of anxiety (particularly generalized anxiety disorder). This is similar to the case with depression in which the symptoms and the self-report of the condition may vary although the underlying mechanism may demonstrate consistencies from one individual to the next.

Anxiety disorders can be categorized into the following disorders:

- Generalized anxiety disorder
- Panic disorder
- Specific phobias
- Obsessive-compulsive disorder
- Post-traumatic stress disorder

- Selective mutism

- Separation anxiety disorder

- Situational anxiety

- Social anxiety disorder

- Agoraphobia

There is also a relatively archaic term called panphobia, which refers to a persistent fear or dread of everything. Panphobia is not considered a specific phobia in the medical community. In fact, it can be considered an aspect or dimension of generalized anxiety disorder as individuals with generalized anxiety do not have generally have fears or worries of something specific (as is the case with specific phobias). Panphobia, therefore, will not be specifically explored in this book, although generalized anxiety disorder will be more thoroughly examined in this chapter and the next.

Anxiousness is a complex modality to examine because it defies attempts to generalize it. Understanding anxiety, therefore, begins with diving it into its constituent parts (or disorders) and examining how these conditions are both distinct and similar to one another. For the person dealing with a spouse or partner who may be suffering from anxiety, part of the process of recognizing anxiety will involve trying to figure out whether your partner has generalized anxiety disorder or something else.

Although this book is intended to be used by anyone interested in this disorder in the relationship setting, when the term anxiety is used generalized anxiety disorder will usually be meant unless otherwise specified. Most readers will be at least superficially familiar with conditions like post-traumatic stress disorder, obsessive-compulsive disorder and the like, and will, therefore, be able to recognize how these conditions can differ superficially from generalized anxiety disorder, although this subject will be explored in more detail later.

Generalized anxiety disorder or GAD is characterized by six months of significant worries over many different activities, which is dysfunctional for the individual. The dysfunctionality aspect of GAD involves the difficulty the individual faces in managing these worries on their own. In addition to the generalized worry, men and women with GAD should also experience three of the following (although only one in the list is required in children):

- Sleep difficulty
- Muscle tension
- Difficulty concentrating
- Easily exhausted
- Irritability
- Restlessness

Because anxiousness can actually be symptomatic of other potentially more life-threatening conditions, a diagnosis of generalized anxiety disorder requires that the symptoms associated with the unease are not caused by a medication or another condition. For a diagnosis of generalized anxiety disorder, it is also required that the symptoms, associated with the anxiety do not meet criteria for another anxious disorder, such as those previously listed.

These are the criteria for GAD as required by the most recent Diagnostic and Statistical Manual for Mental Disorders (DSM-5). This is the standard that is used to diagnose mental illness in the United States and other countries that base their systems on the American system. There is also the ICD system that is used in many European jurisdictions. The ICD-10 criteria include six months of anxiety along with four other systems, including somatic complaints like difficulty swallowing and tingling. For the ICD-10 diagnosis of anxiety, the individual also must not meet criteria for other anxiety disorders like obsessive-compulsive disorder and panic disorder.

Although all anxiety disorders can be grouped under the umbrella term "anxiety" (and they often are), there are aspects of GAD that render it a convenient subject for study. About one-third of people with GAD are believed to have a genetic cause for their condition. Generalized anxiety disorder can be triggered in these people by a life event that sets off the constellation of symptoms and experiences that characterizes this condition.

The Causes of Anxiety

Anxiety disorders like GAD can have a number of other causes besides genetics. Risk factors for anxiety include substance abuse, gender, and life experiences. For example, individuals who have had a traumatic experience early on in life may be more likely to develop generalized anxiety disorder. In this regard, GAD is similar to some of the other disorders like post-traumatic stress disorder that are often linked to a specific inciting event.

From the standpoint of a relationship, it is important for a partner not to blame themselves for their partner's anxiousness even when it seems that something they did may have triggered a symptom. Later in this book, we will discuss things that the reader can do to prevent their partner's condition from getting worse, but it is fundamentally important for the reader to recognize that the ultimate cause of the anxiousness in their partner is something that has nothing to do with them. This is also true for the person with an anxiety disorder reading this book. Although your spouse or partner may do something to set you off, your partner's behaviors are not the essential cause of your symptoms.

There are comorbidities associated with generalized anxiety disorder. These are conditions that commonly co-occur with anxiousness. Perhaps the most important comorbidity with anxiousness is depression, with nearly 60% of people with major depressive disorder also having an anxiety disorder.

About a third of these people have generalized anxiety disorder while others have conditions like agoraphobia, social phobia, and panic disorder. Although this comorbidity may represent an additional burden for the anxious person, the overlap in treatment for these conditions (such as medication and therapy) represent a unique opportunity to kill two birds with one stone so to speak. Other conditions that commonly co-occur with anxiousness include substance abuse disorder, irritable bowel syndrome, and attention deficit hyperactivity disorder (ADHD).

Differential Diagnosis for Anxiety

The differential diagnosis of conditions that may present with anxiousness includes a large list of medical conditions. This should come as no surprise to the reader. Because anxiety is directly tied to disorders in brain chemistry with a specific role for neurotransmitters, any condition that impacts the brain pathway associated with the fight or flight response or the neurotransmitters involved in this response may present with anxiousness. The differential diagnosis for anxiousness will, therefore, include conditions like the following:

- Diabetes
- Endocrine disorders
- Vitamin and mineral deficiencies
- Cardiovascular disease
- Gastrointestinal disease
- Blood disorders
- Nervous system diseases including multiple sclerosis
- Medication

Chapter 2:
Anxiety Disorders

Anxiety is an emotional state characterized by the experience of fear or worry. Although many people in the United States use the term to refer to generalized anxiety disorder or GAD, several disorders are marked by the fear pathway associated with the emotion of worry. The fear associated with anxiousness is a part of the fight or flight pathway that serves as one of the two major functions of the sympathetic nervous system, part of the autonomic nervous system.

What this means, holistically speaking, is that most anxiety disorders can be thought of as an unnecessary or exaggerated action of the sympathetic nervous system's fight or flight response. The fight or flight response involves a number of body changes that are mediated by epinephrine (also called adrenaline) and which involve the action of other hormones like cortisol. Cortisol is released in response to stress and is involved in a number of important activities (including suppression of activities). The release of cortisol in response to stress triggers the body to release glucose into the bloodstream, to suppress the immune system, and to decrease the formation of bone.

What this means is that although fight or flight can be important in conditions of actual danger, when there is no danger, this fight or flight can be dysfunctional and unhealthy. Indeed, individuals who are anxious or stressed are found to have higher levels of cortisol, which leads to subjective feelings of discomfort, actual physical complaints like headaches or stomach aches, and can lead to health problems down the line like diabetes.

In reality, anxiousness and fear are closely related. Although fear itself is not dysfunctional, anxiety is considered dysfunctional as it is considered to be an emotional state characterized by too much fear, as opposed to merely fear due to a real trigger. Anxious persons are, therefore, those people who experience fear when it is unnecessary, and this is true of people with GAD as well as people with other disorders like panic disorder and obsessive-compulsive disorder.

What the person dealing with a spouse or partner with anxiousness should know is that not all experiences of this condition are the same. There are similarities between the different disorders that psychiatrists and medical professionals characterize as anxiety disorders, but they are distinct enough to merit separate diagnostic criteria in the DSM and ICD systems. An important step that the spouse or partner of an anxious person needs to make is to, therefore, decide if their significant other has symptoms of anxiety and then to determine whether they think the problem is GAD or another condition. Although the diagnosis of the condition will be left to the doctor (as it should be), GAD is distinguished from other anxiety disorders in that it does not occur in response to a specific trigger. This can be important for the partner to recognize as their goal ostensibly is to support their partner through their symptoms and not to make the condition worse.

The Fear Pathway

We have referred repeatedly to the fear pathway in this book in reference to the fight or flight pathway that is triggered by anxiety. This fear pathway was postulated based on similarities between individuals with different anxiety disorders and based on an understanding of hormones like epinephrine (adrenaline) that were known to be associated with the fight or flight response. As readers are likely to know if they have read this far, the fight or flight pathway is a natural response to danger. The issue in anxious individuals is that this fight or flight pathway is triggered in conditions where there is no danger or conditions in which most people would not respond in this way.

The fear pathway refers to the neural signaling pathway in the brain that triggers a reaction in the body. Although this pathway involves neurotransmitters and hormones like epinephrine, norepinephrine, and cortisol, it is actually a fairly complex pathway that involves several steps mediated by several different hormones and neurotransmitters. A key (and little known to most people) area of the brain involved in this pathway is the amygdala. The amygdala is located within the temporal lobes of the brain, an area associated with visual memory and emotion. It has been noted by researchers that anxiety disorders like PTSD have a strong emotional component that often distinguishes them from the typical experience of fear.

As we currently understand it, a stimulus in the environment stimulates the amygdala, and this stimulation is followed by the release of the hormone ACTH by the pituitary gland. The adrenal gland is stimulated practically at the same time and it releases epinephrine. Epinephrine (adrenaline) in concert with cortisol leads to the metabolic and body changes that allow a person to respond appropriately to a threat. There is an increase in glucose and fatty acids in the bloodstream as well as a shift away from the body processes that may unnecessarily deplete energy (like bone formation). The fear pathway, therefore, leads to an individual that has the energy and alertness to be able to respond to danger.

But imagine what happens when this fear pathway is activated when there is no danger. A person who is activated in this case will be experiencing all of the bodily changes that someone who is in actual danger would experience. A person with a specific phobia, PTSD, or OCD will experience a persistent worry or fear in response to what is essentially an innocuous trigger, while someone with generalized anxiety disorder may experience this fear in response to many triggers or no specific trigger at all. This fear pathway represents a state that is meant to only be activated briefly in times of danger. By constantly being in a state of heightened fear, a person is not only taxing the brain to an unnecessary degree, but they are adversely impacting their health in multiple ways.

The purpose of the fight or flight response is to render the man or woman able to respond to danger, and it does this in four main ways. These mechanisms can be summarized as follows:

- Release of energy molecules into the bloodstream and increase in blood pressure
- Increase in tension in the muscles to encourage muscle strength and speed
- Diversion of blood flow away from the gut and other areas to the muscle
- More efficient blood clotting to accommodate

situations where bodily trauma may occur

Therefore, the fight or flight response serves a very important function in enhancing human survival in times of danger. This mechanism evolved in human beings for a reason, and it has not been removed from humans by natural selection in the last several thousand years of civilization because it serves an important purpose. This is part of what makes anxiety so difficult to treat and to understand. Fear serves a purpose in human beings and anxiety, therefore, represents the exaggeration of what is essentially an important response.

The reasons why anxiousness is more common in certain groups like women and Westernized people is a continuing subject of debate, a subject which was touched on in the first chapter. These persistent questions may never be answered, but it is likely that there is a biological or hormonal component related to anxiety prevalence that is not fully understood. It is known that the fear pathway involves several hormones and signaling molecules and it is possible that other hormones may activate this pathway covertly. Also, the experience of anxiousness is closely associated with individual experiences of trauma. Experiences of real or imagined trauma may be working to cause anxiety on a societal level in ways that are not fully understood at present.

What is important to know from the standpoint of anxious conditions is some of the bodily changes that are associated with the activation of the fear pathway in the brain. Links between these changes and some of the symptoms of worry are clear. Some of the changes associated with the fight or flight response include:

- Loss of peripheral vision (tunnel vision)
- Relaxation of bladder
- Loss of hearing
- Blood vessel dilation to increase blood flow to the muscles
- Pupillary dilation
- Release of glycogen and flat stores to increase muscular activity
- Inhibition of salivation and lacrimation
- Inhibition of digestive processes
- Tightening of sphincters in several areas of the

body

- Constriction of some blood vessels to increase blood pressure
- Increase in heart rate and respiratory rate
- Visible symptoms like flushing, paling, shaking

As stated earlier, these symptoms represent necessary changes the body must undergo in order to increase energy supply, reduce energy consumption on unnecessary activities, and increase the ability of the body to fight and engage in muscular action in general. It should not be difficult for the reader to see how disturbing these symptoms must be in someone who experiences them commonly and without a real trigger (as is the case in GAD). Although not all anxious people experience all of these symptoms all of the time, these symptoms are disturbing enough that recognizing them is an important part of being able to help another person (or yourself) through anxiety.

Review of Anxiety Disorders

As the reader now understands, the subjective experience of anxiousness involves the activation of the fight or flight pathway either in response to a specific trigger or as a prolonged or general experience. Although this will be explained further below, it might be easier for the reader to think of GAD as forming a contrast to, say, a specific phobia in which a specific trigger (like a snake or a spider) leads to an exaggerated fear response with all of the body changes that go along with that.

The purpose of this chapter is really to augment the first chapter in helping the reader to understand anxiety. In the first chapter, we defined anxiety, were introduced to the diagnosis of GAD, and we ruminated on some reasons why anxiety may be common in some groups than others. This chapter will delve more deeply into anxiousness by familiarizing the reader with the other disorders that constitute the anxious spectrum. This is important to do as "anxiety" does not constitute GAD alone. Indeed, worldwide, about half or less of people experiencing anxiety have GAD with the others having conditions like social phobia, panic disorder, PTSD, specific phobias, and the like. Before we jump into an explanation of the different disorders on the anxiety spectrum, let us review the conditions that commonly fall into this grouping.

- Generalized anxiety disorder
- Panic disorder
- Specific phobias
- Obsessive-compulsive disorder
- Post-traumatic stress disorder
- Selective mutism
- Separation anxiety disorder
- Situational anxiety
- Social anxiety disorder
- Agoraphobia

The reader is not expected to become an expert on all of these conditions. There are healthcare professionals who never reach the level of becoming an expert on these conditions. The goal here is for the reader to understand the conditions well enough that they are able to experience sympathy for the men and women with these conditions, and also to be able to assist in making the diagnosis of an anxiety disorder in someone close to them like a spouse or a partner.

Generalized Anxiety Disorder

Generalized anxiety disorder or GAD is perhaps the most well-known diagnosis on this list. It is estimated that GAD is the most common disorder on the spectrum, although it probably represents less than half of all cases of anxiety. GAD is characterized by six months of excessive worry that causes dysfunction in the life of the anxious individual. The worry is also experienced in tandem to other complaints that characterize the feeling of anxiousness, including difficulty sleeping, irritability, and exhaustion. An important part of diagnosis GAD in both the DSM V and ICD-10 is making sure that the anxious symptoms cannot be related to a specific trigger and ruling out related conditions like panic disorder.

Panic Disorder

Panic disorder is a debilitating condition that is associated with panic attacks. These panic attacks are associated with an intense feeling of fear along with body complaints that include difficulty breathing, a sense of terror, sensation of heart thudding or a heart abnormality (palpitations), shaking, sweating, and other complaints. Panic disorder is not uncommon as an estimated three percent of the population will experience a panic attack at some point in their life. Panic attacks are more common in women than in men.

Panic disorder is diagnosed by the occurrence of repeated and unexpected panic attacks. Panic disorder is associated with a fear of panic attacks and may occur with agoraphobia or without it. Some psychiatrists say that caution should be exercised in diagnosing panic disorder in depressed individuals as these may be occurring secondarily to depression. Panic attacks can also be triggered by medications and medical conditions. What is important for the spouse or partner of someone who experiences panic attacks to know is just how uncomfortable and debilitating these attacks can be. Individuals experiencing attacks of this nature need your sympathy and support.

Specific Phobias

Specific phobias are much more common than people realize. Indeed, it is estimated that nearly one in ten Americans will experience a specific phobia episode at some point. This appears to represent a prevalence greater than most countries, including other Western countries. Many readers will be familiar with specific phobia, possibly because they have themselves experienced anxiety related to a phobia. A specific phobia is a feeling of intense fear related to a specific trigger. Specific phobias are commonly divided into types based on the category that the trigger belongs to. A common division into types includes animal type, situational type, environment type, blood/injury type.

The list of phobias is so long that the discussion of them could easily take up an entire book. Indeed, a book could be written for each phobia. A thorough discussion of phobias is outside the scope of this particular book, although we will say that the trigger should always cause fear and worry and that the individual should avoid the trigger in order for the diagnosis of specific phobia to be met. Some well-known specific phobias include:

- Achluophobia: fear of the dark
- Acrophobia: fear of heights
- Ailurophobia: fear of cats
- Arachnophobia: fear of spiders

- Belonephobia: fear of needles
- Catoptrophobia: fear of mirrors
- Chiroptophobia: fear of bats
- Chronophobia: fear of time advancing forward
- Chronomentrophobia: fear of clocks and timepieces
- Coulrophobia: fear of clowns
- Cynophobia: fear of dogs
- Dentophobia: fear of dental professionals
- Dysmorphophobia: fear of an imagined or real body defect
- Enocholophobia: fear of crowds
- Equinophobia: fear of horses
- Gamophobia: fear of marriage
- Glossophobia: fear of speaking
- Gymnophobia: fear of nudity
- Gynophobia: fear of women
- Hemophobia: fear of blood
- Herpetophobia: fear of reptiles
- Necrophobia: fear of dead people or death

- Nosocomephobia: fear of hospitals
- Numerophobia: fear of numbers
- Ophidiophobia: fear of snakes
- Ornithophobia: fear of birds
- Pteromerhanophobia: fear of flying
- Spectrophobia: fear of mirrors
- Tokophobia: fear of pregnancy or childbirth
- Triskaidekaphobia: fear of the number thirteen
- Venustraphobia: fear of attractive women
- Xenophobia: fear of foreigners or strangers
- Zoophobia: fear of animals

Although Dysmorphophobia is grouped under phobias for the purpose of expounding on the subject of specific phobias, by most diagnostic manuals a fear of real or perceived body defect is usually diagnosed as Body Dysmorphic Disorder, which is a separate disorder from the specific phobias and which falls into the obsessive-compulsive disorder spectrum. This disorder can impact men as well as women, with men commonly experiencing dissatisfaction with their body size, shape, or muscle mass. In the context of muscularity in men, Body Dysmorphic Disorder is sometimes referred to informally as "bigorexia."

Obsessive-compulsive Disorder

Obsessive-compulsive disorder was characterized as an anxiety disorder in the previous version of the Diagnostic and Statistical Manual, although it is not listed as such in the DSM V, the current version. It remains classed as an anxiety disorder in the ICD-10. Individuals with OCD have obsessions and compulsions that they must complete and which cause dysfunction in their lives. Obsessions in this context are thoughts that are intrusive and which cause distress while compulsions are ritualized behaviors that must be performed repeatedly to alleviate stress.

Individuals with OCD know that their obsessions and compulsions are dysfunctional and they struggle with this awareness in their daily lives. There has been much postulation about where OCD comes from and the general path that OCD takes in the lives of afflicted individuals. OCD appears to be more common in children than in adults. A small percentage of people with OCD will eventually experience recovery from their symptoms while about half of all OCD-affected individuals will experience some improvement.

Post-traumatic Stress Disorder

Post-traumatic stress disorder or PTSD is one of the most studied of the disorders on this list. This is in part because of the debilitating nature of the condition, while it is also related to the tendency for this disorder to be not uncommon in members of the military community. Like OCD, PTSD is technically no longer considered an anxiety disorder as it has been moved to its own category in the most recent iteration of the DSM. This is a controversial move as PTSD is a disorder whose study shed light on the fight or flight pathway, the fear response, and the amygdala: the triad of fear that has increased greatly the understanding that medical professionals have about PTSD.

Individuals with PTSD experience a specific spectrum of symptoms in relation to their condition, including reliving their experiences in the form of flashbacks, avoidant behaviors to reduce exposure to triggers, and hypervigilance. PTSD is believed to result from traumatic experience that causes the fear pathway through the amygdala to be stimulated in what may be considered ordinary or non-threatening situations. These traumatic situations may include combat, bullying, natural disasters, or serious accidents (like a motor vehicle accident). Although treatment will be discussed later, PTSD is one of those disorders that often benefits from therapy rather than medication alone.

Selective Mutism

Unlike some of the other disorders on the list, selective mutism has managed to survive the great reclassification of the DSM that has caused some of the other disorders to no longer be classified as anxiety disorders in the United States (although most continue to be classed as such by the ICD system). Selective mutism is a condition in which an individual who has the capacity for speech is unable to speak to certain people or in specific situations. An important component of selective mutism is that individuals are mute even in cases where their mutism may result in embarrassment, punishment, or other consequences.

Selective mutism is unique among the disorders on the spectrum in that the most obvious symptom is not a clear manifestation of anxiousness, although the mutism itself is believed to have an underlying anxious cause. In order to be diagnosed as such, selective mutism must cause dysfunction in the daily life of the individual impacted by it. Also, the mutism must not be attributable to other disorder of communication like schizophrenia or autism spectrum disorders.

Separation Anxiety Disorder

Separation Anxiety Disorder is a condition characterized by feelings of worry associated with being separated from people to whom the individual has formed an attachment. Previously a disorder of children, separation anxiety can be diagnosed in adults if the condition can be shown to have a duration of six months or longer. In children, a duration of four weeks is sufficient to make the diagnosis. Separation anxiety disorder or SAD is associated with an exaggerated display of distress when the individual is faced with separation from home or from people to whom they are attached. An inherent assumption in Separation Anxiety Disorder is that the emotions are excessive and dysfunctional when the child's (or adult's) age and developmental level are taken into account.

Situational Anxiety

Situational anxiety refers to symptoms of worry that occur in response to new events or a specific event. Situational anxiety can be characterized by excessive worry about the event or the upcoming change, or the individual may experience panic attacks when placed in a specific situation. Situational anxiety, therefore, can have features of other disorders like panic disorder, social phobia, GAD, or specific phobias. The situations that trigger anxiousness in these individuals would not be expected to cause this symptom in others.

Social Anxiety Disorder or Social Phobia

Social phobia is an disorder characterized by fear or discomfort associated with being in social situations. Some people with social phobia experience symptoms of anxiety or worry in response to specific social situations like parties or public speaking engagement, while most people with social anxiety disorder or social phobia experience these symptoms in a generalized fashion. Although it may be difficult for significant others or family members to fully relate to these feelings and symptoms, this condition can be very debilitating for the person affected. As in specific phobias, people with social phobia will often attempt to avoid the trigger of their symptoms.

Agoraphobia

Agoraphobia refers to anxious symptoms related to being in public places such as crowds. Although this disorder is often rationalized as a fear of being unable to escape from certain situations where there are a lot of people and where there is a lack of movement, agoraphobia is related to panic disorder in which the symptoms can be triggered suddenly and may be only vaguely related to a "rational" fear. People with agoraphobia may engage in behaviors designed to avoid situations that trigger their symptoms, which, as the reader has seen, can be construed as a coping mechanism for the anxiety, but one which reinforces the anxiousness to some degree.

Because there are similarities between anxiety disorders, even those disorders like post-traumatic stress disorder that have been separated from the other disorders in the most recent version of the Diagnostic and Statistical Manual, the reader can get a sense of the gestalt that underlies anxiousness and the impact that this feeling can have on a relationship. Anxious persons can be withdrawn like depressed individuals, or they can experience the obsessions and compulsions of OCD that makes daily life for them difficult and interacting them often fraught with difficulties.

What the reader should take away from this chapter is that anxiety disorders are characterized by activation of the fight or flight response, whether it is in response to a specific trigger as is the case with phobias or as part of a generalized hyperawareness or sensitivity as may be seen with GAD or post-traumatic stress disorder. Having compassion for someone with anxiousness and learning to accept some of their behaviors (or at least tolerating them) is perhaps the first step to successfully dating someone with anxiousness, a subject that will be explored further in the following chapter.

Chapter 3:
Dating Someone with Anxiety

Anxious feelings can be intensified in romantic relationships. A person who is anxious deals with lingering worries and fears. Recall the point that was made about post-traumatic stress disorder (PTSD). Although the Diagnostic and Statistical Manual has separated this particular diagnosis out from other anxiety disorders and placed it on a trauma spectrum, the trauma that can trigger PTSD is not dissimilar from the triggers that anxious people face.

A person with PTSD can be triggered by events in their environment that would not normally be triggering for other people. They can be triggered by loud sounds, unfamiliar environments, crowds, unfamiliar people, and the like. Although an individual with an anxiety disorder, GAD, for example, is likely to have different triggers, the basic idea remains the same. Individuals with anxiousness often have a hyperawareness just as people that have suffered traumatic experiences do.

An anxious person may react to an interaction more intensely than someone who does not suffer from excessive worry might because they may perceive words or actions to have a meaning that they may not have. What makes anxiousness trying for the sufferer (and the medical professional) is that it is not always simple to tease out what is a legitimate worry and what represents an excessive or dysfunctional worry. Think about the case of someone with PTSD. A person who has been engaged in combat (in war, for example) is likely to attach significance to loud sounds, the sight of weapons, or conflict to a degree that someone who has not been engaged in combat has. This does not mean that they are wrong to attach meaning to these things, but they are more keyed into them than someone else has.

Although there is not a common cause for worry, individuals with anxiousness can appear to have intense reactions to things in a way that seems excessive, just as if they had experienced trauma in the past. Some psychiatrists believe that anxiousness may be more common in people that have experienced trauma, although the prevalence of anxiety cannot be fully accounted for by this supposition. Conditions of anxiousness have been found to be more common in Western nations, in women, and it also runs in families. It is not easy to explain all of this in the context of trauma, although a simple rule for someone who is unfamiliar with anxiousness may be to approach anxious men and women as if they had been exposed to trauma.

The idea behind this approach is not to marginalize anxious people or to perceive them as being abnormal in some fundamental way, but really, the point is to help the reader feel sympathy for the anxious individual. Sympathy means having a level of understanding for what the other person is going through as well as feeling a degree of compassion and tolerance for what they are going through. It may be difficult for someone who is not anxious to understand just what it feels like to have persistent worries so thinking about dealing with anxiousness from the standpoint of trauma may help someone to quickly remember to be a little more understanding than they normally would be.

Thinking about anxious individuals as being more keyed into or words and actions is about more than being sympathetic, however. Approaching affairs this way also helps the individual to be conscious of the things that they say and do that might trigger or intensify the reaction of the anxious individual. Just as you may avoid playing a loud rap song rife with gunshot sounds in front of a person with PTSD or avoid taking them to a club filled with people, flashing lights, and garish sounds, you may also want to think about the things that you can do to avoid making your significant other's anxiety worse.

An anxious person may have a tendency to overanalyze, attaching importance to things that to you may seem insignificant. You may suggest doing this or that, or may even provide a long list of possibilities. This may not be the best strategy when interacting with an anxious person because they may potentially obsess about all of the aspects of the options that you have given them, rather than being able to focus on merely one thing.

Having the Right Approach to Anxiety

Some psychiatrists believe that the negative connotations that some people who do not have anxiety can attach to anxiety can make anxiety worse for the significant other, and can make the experience of dealing with anxiousness worse for both individuals in the relationship. These psychiatrists have written much on the idea that the best approach to dealing with anxiousness in the relationship setting is perhaps to be understanding of it and curious about it. Approaching anxiousness from the standpoint of fear increases the likelihood of a negative interaction because you are projecting your own preconceived notions onto the interaction.

Perhaps it helps to think about it like this. We live in an information age. This information age that we live in can be a positive thing, but it can also be a negative thing. Having access to information allows us to educate ourselves on a wide variety of subjects with the click of a mouse or the swipe of a finger. Information of an encyclopedic nature is more easily accessible today than it was in the past. But that is just one aspect of the information age. Another aspect of this societal change is that individuals are now able to communicate with one another in ways that they were not able to before.

This is really an age of instant communication. This instant communication can be used for good, or it can be used for not so good. This will all become clear in a moment. Let us say that someone decides to go to a local restaurant in their community. For whatever reason, this person (or couple) has a bad experience. Perhaps the waiter is a little short with them, maybe the food is cold, or perhaps the food was not to their liking. This individual (or couple) then uses social media to tell everyone about their bad experience. Now others will either avoid the restaurant completely or perhaps be inclined to see their own future experience negatively because they have already been clued into the negative experience of others.

But if you were to go to the restaurant from the standpoint of curiosity, rather than with your own preconceived notions about the restaurant, then perhaps your experience would be different. Perhaps before the bad review you had often walked past the restaurant and seen all the satisfied people sitting inside or coming out of the restaurant. Perhaps the restaurant serves cuisine that you are particularly fond of. Rather than going to the restaurant with the notion of confirming the negative ideas that you have heard, the best approach is perhaps to eat there with curiosity: fulfilling a long interest that you had in eating in this particular establishment.

By the same token, it is important not to approach interactions with anxious people (or a particular anxious person) with preconceived notions based on stories that you have heard. Maybe you have heard that a particular person is "difficult" (or whatever not particularly nice word people choose to refer to someone else that they do not like). Rather than assume that what you heard is true (and it very well might not be) and use that information to guide your interaction with the person, perhaps keep an open mind. Maybe it was really the other person who was difficult and the anxious person merely reacted to other person in a dysfunctional way. You never really know that the stories and perceptions that you hear from others are true and when it comes to conditions of mental health it is always a good idea to keep an open mind about things like this.

Approaching anxiousness this way not only allows you to have a better reaction than you otherwise might have, but it also allows you to be the compassionate, considerate human being that you ought to be (and that you want to be). You are reading this book for a reason. You are not reading this book because you are someone who lacks empathy and your goal is to be as inconsiderate to anxious people as possible. If you are reading this book, it is probably because there is someone in your life who suffers from worry and to whom you would like to be more understanding, or because you have the condition yourself and you are interested in how you can navigate the pitfalls that come with being in a relationship.

All relationships are fraught with pitfalls. This is just as true for relationships where one person has a mental health condition as it is for relationships where both partners are ostensibly "normal" individuals. Of course, the argument can be made that no one is really "normal." Society decides what normal is and the men and women who are members of that society all strive to meet that societal notion of normal. If anything, this understanding of the almost arbitrary nature of normalcy should allow you to be a little more sympathetic to anxious individuals or others suffering their own struggles with mental health.

Therefore, the best first thing to remember when it comes to having a relationship with someone with anxiousness is to have a curiosity about their symptoms and a desire to learn more. This allows you to approach the relationship from the standpoint of desiring to learn more about the other person – all the things that make them tick and which presumably drew them to you – rather than embarking on this journey with notions about the other person that are based on limited understanding, hearsay, and the like.

The second thing to remember is an important piece of advice that psychotherapists often tell their clients as a coping mechanism. Men and women all over their world are all dealing with their own troubles. When you meet someone, you do not know what they may be dealing with in their life that may make life more trying for them. Sure, it can be a chore to be understanding of the internal states of others at all times, especially when others, unfortunately, may not be understanding of our own internal states. But by recognizing that others have their own internal emotional states and struggles and that our own emotional states are different, we are able to draw a line between the dysfunction that others experience and the potential dysfunction that we may infuse into our own lives.

That is just an introduction to the advice that psychotherapists give; we have not gotten to the important bit yet. So what is the advice that psychiatrists give their patients as a coping mechanism? You should not allow another person's emotional state dictate your own. This is not advice that is given specifically for dealing with individuals with anxiousness. Indeed, this is general advice for navigating life in a world that may seem to be increasingly going off the deep end. This is a way for you to maintain your sanity.

What this piece of advice is getting at is that you should not allow another person's anger, sadness, rage, or whatever reactionary emotion that they are having impact on how you feel and act. This is not to say that anxious individuals will necessarily have negative emotions and inspire negative emotions, although this can sometimes happen. The idea here is that your mental state is distinct from that of the person that you are dealing with, so you need to be able to say: "This person is upset right not for whatever reason and I am okay with that. There is no reason for me to become upset."

What this does is it allows you to remain calm and free of worries even in the context of dealing with someone who may be angry, worried, or otherwise upset. It can be easy to react to the emotional state of others by becoming as emotional as they are. This is a sort of defense strategy and, in fact, this sort of strategy may be more common in individuals who have anxiousness, depression, a personality disorder, or another condition that impacts how the individual sees the world and interacts with it.

In other words, anxious individuals tend to react to things in ways that are dysfunctional. They may interpret things that you say and do as threatening, challenging, offensive, or in other ways that are interpreted by their brain as not benign. The last thing you need to do is to respond to their own emotional reaction in a similar fashion. If you find that you have upset them by something that you have said or done, it is not beneficial to anyone for you to become upset too. The best thing to do is to recognize that the other person is upset for whatever reason and then recognize that you are not upset and there is no reason for you to become upset.

This approach accomplishes a number of things. The first thing that it does is it prevents you from worsening the anxiety or emotion of the other person by responding in kind. If your partner is upset, your becoming upset is not going to make matters any better. The second thing that this approach does is it actually diffuses a situation (in most cases). If you remain calm and are able to project an image of serenity and happiness, this may clue the anxious person in that things are okay and that there is no reason for them to be defensive.

Of course, it is not easy to always be the person who is responding to anger, aggression, or any other emotional reaction by always being the person who remains calm. You may begin to feel that you are being taken advantage of because you are the person who is always expected to be calm and level-headed while the other person is a raging maniac. But it is important to remember here that an anxious or traumatized person tends to respond defensively or emotionally to ambiguous or unfamiliar situations. In other words, if you apply this strategy of remaining calm in the face of the other person's emotion long enough that person should eventually see that you (and the little things that you do) are not threatening and that there is no need for them to respond defensively to you.

Do We Live in a Traumatized Society?

Of course, this approach to the subject of dealing with anxiousness opens up a few interesting doors. The question of why worry is more common in Western society than non-Western societies or more common in women than in men suggests that there may be a role that trauma is playing in the prevalence of anxiety. And this is not real trauma in the form of events that have actually happened to one person or another, but imagined trauma.

What are we getting at here? Perhaps anxiousness is so prevalent because television, media, social media, or even enhanced communication have made us all into traumatized individuals. If you lived on a farm somewhere where everyone was honest, kind, and nothing bad ever happened would you be an anxious person responding to every person that you meet as threatening and dangerous. Probably not. Could it be that people in the West have issues with anxiousness because we are traumatized by the things that we see on television news that make us hypersensitive to other people? Could it be that all of the gossip and distorted stories that are spread on social media has made Americans and other Westerners traumatized by instilling fear in us?

Recall that anxiousness is an emotion characterized by excessive worry or an exaggerated sense of fear. During an anxious episode or a panic attack, the fight or flight response is activated, leading to a heightened state characterized by muscle tension, increased energy, and other bodily changes. This fight or flight response is part of the sympathetic nervous system and is designed to make men and women able to fight and survive if they need to.

A society of anxious people means that we are all geared up to fight even though there is nothing real triggering our emotion. The key to understanding why Western people may be more anxious and keyed up toward conflict requires recognizing what it is that is different in the West compared to other countries. This is not an easy question to answer as each nation in the West is different, and some nations clearly have less of a problem with anxiousness and stress than others do. For example, the Scandinavian nation of Denmark has been described as the "happiest nation on Earth." What makes people in Denmark happier than individuals in other Western nations or in other parts of the world?

The most obvious difference between the West and non-Western nations is technology. Technological advancement has proceeded at a breakneck pace in the West ever since the beginnings of the Industrial Revolution at the end of the 18th century. In reality, the Industrial Revolution was itself part of a long period of small changes that had been building up for several centuries prior to that time. The question then becomes what is it about technology in the West that makes the West a more anxious place to live than other places are?

This, again, is not an easy question to answer, but it is a significant one in the context of this book, and this chapter in particular. Individuals in the West, and increasingly in non-Western nations, have ways to communicate their anxieties, fears, and emotions instantly. Although individuals may not intend to communicate what they are thinking and how they are feeling for negative purposes, the ambiguity that comes with communicating via text, email, or even over the phone sort of sets the stage for millions (or even billions) of keyed up, anxious people.

The news media uses this as a tactic to get ratings. News stories are produced that are intended to generate fear in the viewer, and the idea is that a viewer who has newly been instilled with fear is more likely to watch than someone who has emotional ambiguity to the subject matter. Why would you watch a program that has no direct meaning to you and which you do not care about emotionally or otherwise? By getting you to feel fear, worry, or concern, the program convinces you to care about the subject matter by getting you to feel a powerful emotion.

So do we live in a society that has been traumatized by sensationalized news programs and distorted or outright untrue information communicated via social media? Some would argue that, yes, we do live in such a society. The days where men and women lived in small communities where they were not exposed to manipulated information from the news or social media, and where everyone knew what was what because they could see it for themselves: those days are long gone in the West. But they may not be long gone in other parts of the world, which is perhaps why anxiety is not as common in these "underdeveloped" places.

So what does that mean for you as the spouse or partner of someone who may be anxious? No, it does not mean that you should move to a deserted island somewhere and try to start over, nice as that may sound. What that means is that you should be conscious of some of the ways that you may be reinforcing your partner's anxious symptoms. Although a later chapter will deal with tips on how to prevent you from worsening your anxiety, the present chapter represents a convenient place to discuss some strategies that you can use to manage the anxiety of a significant other.

Communication is Important (Speak face to face, not via text)

This is an issue that the reader was exposed to in the previous section. An anxious person can attach special significance to words or actions, especially if they are ambiguous. The problem with communicating via email, text, or any other form of communication that is not face to face is that the cues that communicate emotion or intention to the other person are muter or open to misinterpretation when they are not seen or heard. How does someone know what you meant by what you said if they cannot see your face or hear the tone of your voice. A happy-faced emoji or a winking eye emoji just does not cut it. The idea that there are young people growing up today who only know how to communicate this way is frankly terrifying.

Some professionals say that important communication with an anxious person should avoid email and text and focus on other forms of communication, including telephone, but even the telephone can be problematic. Sure, a telephone call can at least convey the familiarity of the other person's voice, but this is still a form of communication that technology that does not quite hit all the points that a face to face conversation. Even Skype cannot do that. When it comes to communication with someone who is anxious, try to keep important communiques face to face if you can.

Learn to Listen

Talking and listening are not the same thing. Just because you are having a conversation with someone, this does not necessarily mean that you are listening. Although it may seem that the anxious person that you are communicating with is not listening either, most likely they are paying very close attention to the words you are saying and the visual cues you are sending. As we have already said, the anxious person is attaching special meaning to your words and actions, so they are likely to be watching and hearing you closely.

This means that if you are interested in having a successful relationship with someone who is anxious, then you need to learn to listen to. This is not merely a tit for tat scenario: listening closely to your anxious partner solely because they are listening closely to you, but if you truly want to understand your partner and you truly want to learn how to correctly interpret their own cues, then you need to start listening and opening your eyes.

Stay Calm

This is a piece of advice that will come to represent a common theme throughout the pages of this book. This was already touched on in the context of recommending that the reader should not respond to the emotions of another person with their own emotion. It is to your benefit to stay calm. Every interaction that you have with someone who is anxious should be approached from a place of calmness and serenity. We all have our stresses. Most people have employment and may come home stressed out from that. It may be difficult for you to be calm when you are stressed yourself.

But the reality is that your relationship with an anxious person is unlikely to be successful if you have difficulty remaining calm. If you are constantly agitated or stressed and are therefore inclined to respond to the tense emotional state of your partner with your own heightened emotions, then your relationship is likely to be fraught with arguments, battles, and emotionality. Some relationships can certainly weather the story that frequent emotional battles represent, but the most successful relationships are based on commonalities, whether that is a common understanding, common goals, or a common appreciation for the value of peace and understanding.

Ask Questions to Understand How Your Partner Feels

Asking questions to understand how your partner is really feeling helps. You are not a clairvoyant and you, therefore, would not be expected to know what your partner is thinking or feeling at all times. It is important to know how your partner feels so that you can support them through whatever they are going through. Also, knowing what your partner is thinking or how they are feeling can help you remain calm because you understand where their worries or emotions are coming from. Ask questions of your partner to get a sense of what they are feeling. You will not regret it.

You Do Not Have to Validate Your Partner's Feelings But At Least Try to Relate to Where They Are Coming From

Some books and websites addressing the question of dealing with an anxious partner say that the significant other needs to put effort into validating the feelings of their partner. That tactic is not recommended in this book because of the reality that the feelings of an anxious person are often dysfunctional and therefore, it may not be the best measure to validate them. As the example of the person with PTSD was meant to illustrate, some of these thoughts or feelings are real, have a purpose, and are not "negative" so to speak, but an anxious person may have thoughts or feelings that may be imagined or otherwise exaggerated.

For example, you may have had lunch with a coworker of the opposite sex at an expensive restaurant as part of a business meeting or a work get-together. Does that mean that you should validate the rage and jealousy that your partner feels when they learn of this meeting via email or text? No. Your first step is to recognize that your partner is upset and your second step is to remain calm. You may understand where the anger and jealousy are coming from, but you can leave it at that.

Observation Is Key to Really Coming to Understand Your Partner

Communication via email or text has really changed the way that we interact with each other. Simple things like observing our significant other to gauge how they are feeling or what they are thinking, these seem to be things of the past. Our interaction with other people, including those close to us, has been reduced to relatively superficial interactions carried out via email or text. If you want to know who your partner is and how they feel, spend time in their company. Even sitting in silence in close proximity with someone can be effective in getting to know them. Technology that has enhanced our ability to communicate cannot take the place of old-fashioned measures like face to face interaction and observation.

Do Not Make Assumptions about Their Anxiety

Do not make assumptions about your partner's anxiousness, for example, assuming that all of the things that they do that you do not like stem from their condition. This is part of the preconceived notions conundrum that we addressed briefly before.

You should approach your relationship with an anxious person from the standpoint of gaining knowledge. You do not know what their subjective experience of being anxious is life, even if you may have yourself experienced anxiousness. What you need to do is be open-minded and take the position of trying to learn more about their condition.

Communicate Things Clearly to Your Partner

It is a good idea to communicate things clearly to your partner rather than leaving room for doubt. We began this chapter by stating that anxiousness can be intensified in romantic relationships. The things that you do and say have special meaning to your spouse or romantic partner, more so than the things that someone they are not linked to in the same way say or do. Therefore, effective communication is very important in the context of anxiousness. An anxious partner may misinterpret things that are not communicated clearly, so it is in your interest to put some effort into how you can communicate well with your partner.

Chapter 4:
The Role of Attachment in Relationships with Anxious Individuals

Attachment theory is a model in psychological that seeks to understand how humans form bonds with other humans as a model for their relationships that they will have throughout their lives. Although attachment theory does have its antecedents in the psychoanalytical theories of the 19th century, it is essentially a theory that took shape in the 20th century primarily as the result of observations that were made of infants and toddlers and the relationships that they had with adults.

Attachment theory is primarily a model that focuses on the interpersonal relationships that infants and toddlers form. These attachments are important because they set the stage for how the toddler (and future adult) interacts with others and perceives their environment. It was observed relatively early in the 20tjh century that young children who were deprived of attachment during formative years of their lives seemed to have difficulty interacting with others and forming relationships later on in life.

It should be remembered that attachment theory, along with other psychoanalytic and behavioral theories, took shape at a time when the world (particularly the Western world) was rife with various dramatic social changes. Men and women were moving from rural areas into cities; people of all ages were working in factories or other establishments in urban areas, war was common in some areas which left many communities devastated. In short, the fabric of society was changing in ways that were apparent and which could be conveniently observed by anyone who was paying attention.

The purpose of this chapter is to help the reader understand the role that anxiousness can play in a relationship by teaching them about attachment. It has been argued that some anxious individuals behave as if they have suffered trauma. Certainly, some individuals with anxiety disorders may have suffered real trauma and this may have contributed to their condition, but even in cases where individuals have experienced no known trauma there may be the equivalent of trauma in the form of an insecure attachment that they had with their parent long before they were old enough to remember such interactions.

This knowledge of attachment will help the spouse or partner of an anxious person navigate their relationship. They will be able to do this by understanding how they are perceived by their partner in ways that someone unfamiliar with attachment theory will not understand. As in other areas of discussion pertaining to worry in relationships, the goal here is to aid the reader in feeling compassion for their partner, but also to give them real skills that they can use.

Attachment theory is essentially a model that focuses on the relationships that infants and toddlers have with the important adults in their lives, but the theory has been expounded upon to make deductions about adult relationships. This theory is usually referred to as attachment theory for adults. It is not the goal of this chapter. This chapter focuses on how the relationships of childhood and infancy dictate relationships that are had later on, essentially forming a type of trauma that is played out in the relationships that anxious people have throughout their lives.

Types of Attachment

One of the earliest individuals to explore the idea of attachment as it is understood today was John Bowlby writing in the mid-20th century. It had been observed earlier in the century that children that were deprived of time with or affection from their mother's experienced problem that seemed to be clearly linked to these deprivations. Bowlby was also influenced by other psychologists and behavioral biologists like Konrad Lorenz who were forming general theories about how animals form attachments.

For those of you unfamiliar with Konrad Lorenz, he was a biologist who explored various aspects of animal behavior. In particular, Lorenz was famous for his studies on imprinting in which he showed that a flock of ducks can be taught to see a human being as their parent and to follow them if they are exposed to this human being at an important formative moment. Lorenz's work was so important that he received a Nobel Prize for it 1973. His work still forms the basis for how animal behavior is understood and researched today.

In terms of attachment theory, the important idea is that young humans form attachment with older adults (usually a parent, called a primary caregiver) in order to enhance their chances of survival and as a model for the relationships that they will have later on. As most readers can probably gather, human beings are pretty much useless in the early years of their life: require care and protection from their caregivers. Infant attachment is, therefore, a behavior that evolved to enhance the survival of the human species. By seeking attachment from a caregiver, an infant engages in a bond that is beneficial both to the individual and to the species.

It is easy to focus on attachment solely in infants and take for granted the role that attachment plays later in life. Individuals that are insecurely attached to their primary caregivers (which will be explained later) will tend to approach their interactions with other individuals from the standpoint of fear and danger. It is interesting to explore the idea that anxiousness on a societal level may be on the rise because of a society-wide problem with attachment during this formative period though this is an idea that has not been actively researched. Studies in the field tend to focus exclusively on the implications of childhood attachment in children and the implications of adulthood attachment in adults.

What is important to understand as a precursor to a study of attachment is what attachment is and how it works. Before Bowlby, many psychologists believed that the behavior of infants and toddlers (essentially children under the age of two in this context) was a result of a complex fantasy world that existed in the minds of children and from which adults were cut off. This fantasy idea has basically been replaced by the attachment model, which recognizes the role that adults play in interacting with children and setting the pattern for behaviors that children see as normal.

Of course today, this type of thinking may seem obvious to people, but it was not always the case. Psychoanalytic theory perhaps went off the deep end a little bit in the 19th and early 20th centuries as it explored some of the more garish aspects of human personality and attributed to people all sorts of subconscious desires and motivations. Attachment theory essentially goes back to the basics when compared to psychoanalytic theories. Our behaviors as adults and our expectations regarding what is normal and what is not date back to the sort of things that we see when we are children.

Therefore, children who see dysfunction relationships between their parents in their formative years may grow up thinking that it is normal for people to interact this way. This even extends to cases of abuse, where one individual may believe that it is normal to be the target of abuse or to perpetrate abuse on another person. This type of thinking is relatively simplistic compared to attachment theory, but it gives the reader a general idea of how patterns that we are exposed to in our formative years set the stage for our behaviors and expectations as adults.

Anxiousness in adults can, therefore, potentially result from defective forms of attachment that occur in the childhood years. Attachment here is essentially the bond(s) that infants form with the adults around them in the period of about 10 months to 18 months. Although infants may seek attachment from their caregivers prior to this, this is the age range that allows psychologists to assess attachment by placing infants in this age range in certain situations, usually called strange situations.

Research in the area has allowed psychologists to identify four major types of attachment. The goal here is not for the reader to develop an in-depth understanding of the different types of attachment but merely to get an idea of how these forms of attachment play out in the behaviors of adults with anxiousness or other conditions. The four types of attachment described by psychologists include:

- Secure attachment
- Anxious-ambivalent attachment
- Anxious-avoidant attachment

- Disorganized attachment

Secure attachment is the prototypical form of attachment that occurs in infants when everything goes right. Attachment is something that develops in infants, but it results from normal, healthy interactions with their primary caregiver. In the case of secure attachment, children have experienced their emotional and physical needs being met by their caregiver, they have experienced affection from their caregiver, and these two things together allow the infant to feel safe and secure in their environment. The safety that a securely attached child feels allows them to safely explore their environment and will eventually lead to their ability to form healthy relationships with others as an adult.

Anxious-ambivalent attachment occurs when an infant feels excessive worry when separated from their caregiver and does not feel reassured when the caregiver returns. This type of attachment can result if the caregiver does meet the emotional and physical needs of the child, or by their behavior (or neglect) is unable to reassure the infant. In short, the relationship with the caregiver is disturbed in such a way that the infant regards their environment with a degree of fear or uncertainty that a securely attached infant would not typically experience.

Anxious-avoidant attachment and disorganized attachment are two additional forms of attachment that result from problems with how the caregiver interacts with the infant. In anxious-avoidant attachment, the child avoids contact with the caregiver, while in disorganized attachment, the child appears to have no attachment bond with their caregiver at all.

Attachment Problems in Anxious Adults

In this book, several theories have been postulated as to why anxiety seems to have high prevalence in the Western world, including countries like the United States where GAD, specific phobias, and other anxious disorders are common. It was suggested in the previous chapter that individuals in the Western world may be exposed to trauma in the form of information from the news media or social media. It was also suggested that new forms of communication may be heightening and exaggerating a preexisting anxiousness that may exist because of other social factors.

The purpose of this chapter is not to further explore this ideology, but to give the reader a concrete sense of where anxiety may be coming from and how they can manage it. In other words, it may help you to think of the anxious person in your life as experiencing one of the dysfunctional forms of child attachment that we mentioned earlier. The idea here is not for you to perceive your significant other as a child (which they are not), but to gain an understanding of how they perceive their world and where that perception comes from.

Again, it may help to perceive the anxious person as traumatized in some way. The anxious-ambivalent child may become upset when their caregiver departs because they are accustomed to their caregiver not allaying their fears or not minimizing the sense of danger that they perceive in their environment. A child in this category will become upset because they perceive their environment as filled with danger and they want someone to handle the danger that they perceive.

An anxious-avoidant child may avoid their caregiver because they perceive a problem with their caregiver. They may have received mixed signals from their caregiver, which has caused them to distance themselves from them. Perhaps the caregiver displayed anger when they should have displayed compassion or joy. Perhaps the caregiver is perceived as dangerous by the child for whatever reason. This will cause the child to be anxious but essentially to show avoidant behaviors.

Someone with exposure to anxious individuals may start to see some of the similarities here. An anxious person may become upset when their significant others leave and may show jealousy and anger when they return. An anxious person may avoid interacting with their significant other, or they may appear not to care when their significant other goes or comes. These behaviors, rather than stemming from an attachment that the anxious person has formed with their spouse or partner ultimately stem from how the anxious person perceives the world because of the basic pattern that was established when they were a child.

How You Can Overcome Attachment Problems in Your Relationship

Psychotherapists use attachment theory as a base from which to understand adults from an essentially psychoanalytical standpoint. In other words, a therapist will seek to understand why their client manifests the sorts of behaviors and symptoms that they manifest and they do this by trying to analyze aspects of the client, including early childhood experiences. The intention is not for the reader to psychoanalyze their spouse or partner but rather to understand how anxious people may be traumatized or disturbed by something which occurred in their early life.

The reader should avoid the psychoanalytical approach when attempting to handle anxiousness in their partner. This is a point that was made before but which it is important to reiterate here. As much as you may desire to help your spouse or romantic partner, you are not their therapist. It is not important for you to ask the questions: "Why are you like this?" or "What happened to you?" Yes, you should be curious about your significant other's anxious symptoms, but that does not mean that you should dive head first into the closet to unearth all of the skeletons lying there. It is enough for you to recognize that something may have happened in your partner's life without knowing all of the gory details that a psychologist would need to know. You are not their psychologist.

The second point to recognize here is the importance of moving forward and how that can be accomplished. Some people like to use the term abandonment issues. Although this is not a term that will be used in this book, the ideas underlying attachment theory essentially represent what some may think of as abandonment. An insecurely attached child never felt appropriately soothed by their parent, either because the parent demonstrated neglect of the child or because the parent was unable to show secure attachment toward the infant.

It is therefore important for you as the spouse or partner of someone with this type of issue not to abandon them or at the very least to be consistent in how you interact with them. Being inconsistent or borderline in your show of love and affection, being manipulative, these are all ways that you instill distrust in your partner and essentially confirm the suspicions that they have about the world. Only a narcissist would play these sorts of games with someone they are supposed to love. If you care about your partner dealing with anxiousness, then your goal should be to show them that they can trust you, that they can rely on you, that they can expect compassion and consistency from you, and that you are not a source of danger.

Over time, this consistency from you may cause them to perceive the world around them differently, which may cause their anxiety to improve. It may be strange to make the comparison, but this is akin to showing someone who is afraid of spiders that spiders are not all bad. Essentially you are showing your significant other that the world is not such a hostile place for them because you are there and you love them. This is an important component of the therapy that a psychotherapist would take with a person with attachment problems and you can do much good work in your relationship by learning from this approach.

Chapter 5:
Treatment for Anxiety

One of the most important questions that someone dealing with anxiousness has to ask is, how do I treat it? This is just as true of someone dealing with their own symptoms as it is of someone dealing with anxiousness in the context of a relationship. Because worry is not a heterogeneous condition, the forms of treatment can take many different forms. The availability of many treatment options is true of many mental health conditions in addition to anxiety, but it is perhaps particularly important in the case of anxiousness because of the many different conditions that can fall under this moniker.

As the reader as seen, the term anxiety is often used to refer to GAD, although this condition is estimated to account for less than half of cases of anxiousness worldwide. In this chapter, the reader will be familiarized with all of the different treatment modalities available for generalized anxiety disorder. At the end of the chapter, a discussion of treatments for other important disorders like specific phobias and panic disorder will be discussed. There also will be a discussion of alternative medicine treatments for anxious symptoms.

Treatment for anxiety can be divided into the four main areas listed below:

- Medication
- Therapy
- Dietary changes
- Alternative medicine

This review of treatment is intended to be used by the reader as a general guide for those treatments that are available. One of the important takeaway points in this book is that anxiety is a condition that the affected individual is dealing with and which the affected individual should find a solution to. The role of the spouse or partner of the anxious person is to provide support for their significant other and to help them navigate the waters of their condition. As much as the spouse or partner of an anxious person may want to guide or steer their partner in the direction they think they should take, it is ultimately the decision of the anxious person what form their treatment should take if they decide to opt for treatment.

When it comes to treatment, there are some differences between anxiety and other conditions of mental health like depression and schizophrenia. In these latter two conditions, the pathways that are believed to contribute to the symptoms of the conditions have been extensively studied. This has led to the development of specific classes of medications intended to treat these conditions. For example, in depression, the role of serotonin in modulating depression has been extensively studied while in schizophrenia, the role of dopamine has been the object of study. Less is understood about anxiousness and the role that neurotransmitters play in modulating it. Anxiousness is often grouped together with depression as anxious symptoms represent a comorbidity that may be seen in as many as 50% of depressed individuals.

The user should use this chapter as a source of education. They should understand the different types of treatments that are available. They should also understand that not all treatments are effective in all individuals. When it comes to anxiousness, although medication is frequently prescribed, the role that counseling plays in treating the anxious condition is perhaps more significant than it is in other common conditions that affect mental health. This is something that the reader should keep in mind. In some anxious disorders, counseling is considered the first line treatment rather than medication.

Medication Treatment for Anxiety

No discussion of medication treatment for anxiousness would be complete without a review of the selective serotonin reuptake inhibitors (SSRIs) and the serotonin-norepinephrine reuptake inhibitors (SNRIs). These two classes of medications are mainstays in the treatment of depression. Indeed, SSRIs are among the most commonly prescribed medications worldwide, regardless of indication. SSRI antidepressants are a billion-dollar industry and the reader has likely seen television commercials for these medications.

It may come as a surprise that these medications are also prescribed for anxious disorders. When it comes to medication treatment, anxiousness is the little brother of depression. The desire to create drugs that are exclusively designed to treat anxiety has not been pursued the way that antidepressant medication has. This may be because of the inherent heterogeneity that is present in anxiety disorders, or it may be because of the perception that medication treatment for anxious symptoms will always be vying with counseling for primacy. Indeed, there is a perception both in the medical community and among the public that depression can be adequately treated with medication while anxiousness represents a different can of worms altogether.

Be that as it may, there are many medications available for the treatment of anxious symptoms. It has already been stated that nearly all of these medications were produced to treat depression, and this is true for the SSRIs and SNRIs. SSRIs, as the name suggests, work by targeting the serotonin reuptake complexes at the synapse. By blocking these proteins, SSRIs are able to increase the concentration of serotonin present in the synaptic junction. SNRIs work by a similar mechanism, but they increase the concentration of both serotonin and norepinephrine at the synapse. Although the reasons why these medications work is not well understood, studies have shown that these two classes are effective in treating people with depression, anxiety, or both.

SSRIs and SNRIs are not the only medication classes available for the treatment of anxiety. Serotonin agonists like Buspirone and benzodiazepines are also commonly prescribed to treat anxiety. Benzodiazepines have become less popular in recent decades because of the risk of addiction and overdose death. Issues that the reader should keep in mind are that medications can be problematic in older adults because of the prevalence of drug interactions in anxiolytics. As the reader shall soon see, counseling and other treatments have been shown to be very effective in the treatment of anxious symptoms, so if medication is not an option, there are typically other options available.

Therapy for Anxiety

Therapy is considered a first-line treatment for anxiety disorders in contrast to other conditions of mental health. Anxious men and women often have an element of consciousness or agency in their disorder, which makes therapy very effective in treating these conditions. This idea of agency in the context of anxiousness may be difficult to understand, but it essentially means that anxious people are often conscious of their condition and the dysfunction that comes with it in ways that other people with mental health conditions are not. As we have seen, individuals with obsessive-compulsive disorder are very conscious that they have a problem, although they generally have great difficulty in breaking the pattern of obsessions and compulsions that characterizes their conditions.

Perhaps the most popular type of therapy for men and women with anxiousness is cognitive behavioral therapy or CBT. CBT essentially addresses the mental or agency component of the disease process in anxious individuals. CBT is a type of psychotherapy that involves recognizing and targeting dysfunctional thought patterns and regulating emotions. This is an important step for anxious people to engage in. Indeed, some anxious people are able to recognize the importance of ceasing their anxious or obsessive thoughts, even without realizing that they are engaging in what is known as cognitive behavioral therapy. Therapy is particularly effective in conditions like specific phobias and OCD where anxious people can easily become locked into a downward spiral of fear, avoidance, and obsession.

Natural Treatments and Alternative Medicine

There are several effective treatments for anxiousness that fall outside the realm of traditional medications and therapy. These include dietary and lifestyle changes, a subject that is being actively studied. Some foods, such as those that contain caffeine are known to exacerbate anxiety. Indeed, some individuals may develop the symptoms of panic disorder solely because of substances consumed in their diet like caffeine. In the realm of lifestyle change, smoking cessation has been shown effective in the treatment of anxious symptoms in some people.

There are several other important remedies for anxiousness that fall outside of the big two categories of treatment. The other forms of treatment that some men and women with anxiousness have found effective include the following:

- Herbal and traditional remedies
- Transcendental meditation
- Aromatherapy

There are many herbal remedies that men and women have tried to help them deal with their symptoms. Many of these remedies have been used by native and aboriginal groups for hundreds or thousands of years. The list of remedies includes St. John's wort, passionflower, kava, and ayahuasca. Although many herbal remedies are readily available in Western countries like the United States, other forms of treatment like kava and ayahuasca are frequently listed as controlled substances in Western countries. Someone interested in using one of these traditional compounds will have to do their research to determine how they can get their hands on them in the community in which they live.

A quick word about transcendental meditation and aromatherapy. Transcendental meditation has been used as a treatment for many different types of mental illness, including anxiety and depression. This type of treatment may be of particular use in anxiety as it focuses on freeing the individual and their mind from those concerns that way it down and keep it attached to the world. Meditation, therefore, can involve a range of techniques that can relax both the body and the mind. Aromatherapy has been studied in the context of worry secondary to another condition, although there is a belief that it can also be effective in primary anxiety disorders.

Chapter 6:
10 Tips to Help You Support Your Partner through Anxiety

One of the most important things that a spouse or partner of an anxious person has to recognize is that their role in the process is as a supporter. It may be the case that you know your significant other better than anyone else, but that still leaves the task of dealing with anxiousness primarily to them rather than to you. This does not mean that you should leave the anxious symtoms to eat away at the person until it damages their life irreparably, but it means that your place in the big picture should be recognized both by you and by your partner.

The role of the supporter is an important one. The goal of this chapter is to provide you with tips that you can use help you fulfill this role in the best way that you can. Sure, sitting on the sidelines can be frustrating sometimes, but a solid supporter is just what your partner or spouse needs right now. And if you are the one dealing with anxiousness, then these tips will help you get an understanding of the sorts of things that your partner can do for you.

Tip 1: Understand that overcoming anxiety is a process (anxiety is not something that someone will snap out of)

Anxiety is not like having the common cold. It is not something that you get and which will you will experience resolution from with the snap of a finger. Anxiety disorders should be thought of as conditions that require treatment. What this means for the significant other of an anxious person is that you should be realistic about your partner's anxiety. They are not going to snap out of their anxiety and it is more than a little unfair of you to expect them to. As a supporter of an anxious person, it is critical to recognize that you will be helping them through the long process of overcoming their illness.

Tip 2: Be conscious of your own dysfunctional thoughts or preconceived notions

Anxiousness is characterized by a cavalcade of dysfunctional thoughts that people often are not conscious that they are having. Unfortunately for the significant others of anxious persons, they can have their own spiral of dysfunctional thoughts that can impact the way that they perceive and interact with their anxious partner. The meaning here is not that the partner is necessarily at risk for worry, but merely that the partner should recognize how their interaction with their partner can be colored by notions that they have about their condition (including subconscious stigma that men and women often have towards conditions of the mind).

Tip 3: Provide reassurance that things are going to turn out all right

One of the most important things that someone supporting someone else through anxiety (or any condition) can do is to provide reassurance that things are going to turn out all right. This does not mean telling a lie. If someone has a terminal illness like stage IV cancer, it is obviously important to recognize exactly what that means. But honest reassurance in the case of anxiousness is a little different. Anxiety can and does frequently get better, so reminding your partner of that can place a positive thought in their head that can be an important part of creating real change in their life.

Tip 4: Encourage your partner to get help

A difficult reality for some partners of anxious people to accept is that it is not their job to steer their partner in the direction they think they should go. We have established that anxiety disorders are conditions that typically do not get better without treatment, but that does not mean that it is your role as their supporter to force them to get treatment or to dictate to them the form that the treatment should take.

Intervention-type maneuvers can be problematic in mental health. This is especially true in the case of anxiousness, where the individual may already be inclined to have a suspicious or fearful approach to others or the world in general. Forcing or cornering your partner into treatment is not a good idea for anxious people. What you can do is educate yourself about the help that is available for their condition and encourage them to get help. That is really all that you can do.

Tip 5: Be patient as your significant other moves through their condition

It is important to be patient when dealing with a person that has a mental health condition and this is just as true of anxiety as it is of other conditions like depression. Recall that anxiety disorders include conditions as divergent as GAD, specific phobias, and obsessive-compulsive disorder. The point here is that some of these conditions can be very debilitating for the individual dealing with and very frustrating for the partner or family member who is around it. For your own sanity (and for the sake of your partner) it is important to be patient. Change will happen slowly and it will help you to keep this in mind.

Tip 6: Provide ongoing education and support to your partner

Being supportive means being someone that your significant other can go to when they need help. Again, the goal here is not to force your partner to do something that they may not be ready to do but to support them as they decide to make a change and take steps towards making that change. As a supportive partner, you can provide ongoing education for yourself about anxiety and related conditions like depression, and you can even find ways to pass this information along to your partner.

As we have discussed in this book, anxious individuals can have exaggerated or otherwise excessive or unnecessary reactions to stimuli, so it is important that you and your partner both recognize that you are occupying a supportive role. If your partner feels that you are attempting to manipulate them or push them in a particular direction, they may begin to mistrust you and avoid you. Therefore, it is important to approach your partner's anxious symptoms from the standpoint of educating both yourself and them on this subject.

Tip 7: Recognize that no one understands your partner's anxiety more than your partner

As much as you may educate yourself about anxiousness, no one is better poised to understand your partner's anxiety than they are. Sure, you may be around them for several hours of the day and you may feel that you may see aspects of their anxiety that they may seem unconscious of, but as you are not experiencing what they are and are not inside their head to know what the triggers are, you perhaps do not understand their condition as well as you might think. Use this as an opportunity to let your partner educate you about their worries, not the other way around.

Tip 8: Be available, not overbearing

It is easy to fall into the trap of being overbearing when you are in a relationship and you notice that your partner needs help with something. You may find that you have an overweening desire to help them, and perhaps you feel that you are able to see matters from a vantage point that they may not see. Even if that is the case, your partner does have the ability and the right to make decisions for themselves. Loved one or not, you do not necessarily have the right to force them to do as you want them to do if they are not a danger to themselves or others. If you are interested in maintaining a loving relationship with your significant other, you should focus on being available when they support rather than overbearing.

Tip 9: Take your partner's comments seriously

One of the ways that you learn the character of your partner's anxiousness (and gain a deep sense of what they are going through) is by talking to them. Your partner's anxiety is just that, their anxiety, and you need to leave it to them to clue you in on how they are feeling and why. Therefore, it is important as a supportive partner to talk to your partner and to exercise active listening. Just as your anxious partner may hang on to your every word, you need to learn to pay attention to your partner's words. When your partner tells you something about themselves or what they are going through, take it seriously.

Tip 10: Remember that empathy is important

Sympathy is a word that many people understand, although they do not always show it. Sympathy involves feeling compassion and tolerance for others, a feeling that comes from a deep understanding of where the other person is coming from. We can show sympathy for others through our words, our actions, or even by our facial expressions. But empathy is something different. Empathy involves sharing the feelings of others: actually experiencing what they are experiencing. Although having true empathy for someone with a mental condition may be fraught with danger, this is something that many partners are able to do and their relationships can be improved through it.

Having empathy for your partner means that you recognize that their anxiety is not just an illness that they are dealing with but in some ways may be part of them. They may have dealt with anxiousness in some way or another for most of their life and they may not understand how to live without their anxious, obsessive, or compulsive behaviors. By truly coming to experience the world the way that they do, you are able to be a real supporter: someone who is able to deal with their highs and lows right along with them.

Chapter 7:
10 Habits That Can Make Your Partner's Anxiety Worse

As the partner of an anxious person, you can play a critical role in alleviating the symptoms of their condition and making life for them (and you) easier. As we have seen, there many different types of anxiousness that have historically been characterized as anxiety disorders, but if we think of worry as an emotion characterized by excessive worry or fear, then we can understand the common thread that often runs through anxiety disorders. We have also seen that some conditions characterized by worry or fear like post-traumatic stress disorder have recently been redefined by psychiatrists (at least in the United States) and may technically be seen today as "anxiety disorders." That being said, anxiety is a common thread in many dysfunctional ways of thinking or behavior patterns and keeping this in mind is an important step that can lead to change.

Regardless of the type of worry your partner faces, you can be of help to them by aiding them in avoiding habits that can make their symptoms worse. These are also habits that you can work into your own life to steer you away from developing anxiousness yourself and to help you interact better with the anxious person in your life. The purpose of this chapter is to equip you with a useful skill. By recognizing these dysfunctional habits, you are able to minimize the impact of your partner's anxiousness and help place your relationship on the road toward being worry-free.

Habit 1: Setting Unattainable Goals

A habit that can certainly make your partner's anxious symptoms worse is setting unattainable goals. This is a habit that the partner too can develop and which can prove unhealthy in your anxiety-fraught relationship. By setting unattainable goals, the anxious person sets themselves up for a whirlwind of emotions that includes worries, fears, and anger. These emotions come from a subconscious realization that the goal may be unattainable resulting in time spent worrying about the outcome, but they also stem from the whole gamut of emotions that ensue when the goal inevitable fails.

As we have seen, anxious people can have intense reactions to things that may not disturb others. Having a plan or a goal fail (especially if it is an important one) can be devastating to even a person without a mental health issue so it is not hard to see why this would be a problem. By setting a reasonable, attainable goal, you and your partner can reduce the anxiousness that comes with reaching for something that cannot be achieved and then having to deal with the consequences that inevitably come along.

Habit 2: Unhealthy Dietary Habits (like excessive smoking or alcohol consumption)

This is an easy habit that an anxious person can drop (although it may be easier in some people than in others). It may actually come as a surprise to some that certain foods or substances can exacerbate worry. There are a number of these products that should be avoided, but the big ones are caffeinated products like coffee and energy drinks, alcoholic beverages, and tobacco-containing products. Do you really want to give your partner who stays up all night worrying about this or that an energy drink or a heaping pot of coffee a few hours before bedtime? Avoiding these substances will help you keep their anxiety from getting worse and maintain your own sanity.

Habit 3: Excessive Use of Social Media

We live in an age of social media addicts and many people do not have a full understanding of just how problematic this can be. We spoke in the first chapter about some of the social causes of anxiousness. Anxious people have a tendency to obsess over things or to blow things out of proportion. When you consider that much of the information that comes from news programs or is posted to social media is exaggerated or designed to inflame the reader or is outright untrue, it should become obvious why social media can be a problem.

It is a good idea to steer your partner away from using social media if you can. It is also a good idea for you to avoid using social platforms in front of them (or at all). Another part of this is using forms of communication other than face to face. This is something that was discussed earlier on. By limiting your conversation to standard, old-fashioned face to face communication, you can prevent the worries and fears that come from unclear or misinterpreted messages.

Habit 4: Depriving Yourself of Sleep

Sleep deprivation can exacerbate the condition of someone dealing with mental health concerns. This is true of anxiety as well as other conditions like depression, bipolar disorder, and the like. The idea here is that the brain needs sleep in order to function normally and to maintain the body in homeostasis. Although scientists are actually engaged in an active debate as to why precisely sleep is so important, the value of sleep in individuals with mental health concerns is widely acknowledged. Do yourself and your partner a favor and try not to deprive them of sleep. Indeed, encourage them to get about eight hours a night.

Habit 5: Not Getting Enough Exercise

Exercise is not only important in keeping your body in tiptop shape, but it also releases endorphins that cause people to feel happy and energetic. Indeed, it has been argued that the sedentary lifestyle of modern people has impacted us in a number of negative and problematic ways, and the impact that being sedentary can have on the mind is often overlooked. You can help your significant other reduce their anxiety by encouraging them to exercise and by making sure that you are not the cause of why they are not getting enough exercise.

Habit 6: Not Being Honest About How You Are Feeling

A habit that anxious people share with depressed people is that sometimes they are not honest about how they are feeling. They may say that they are fine when in reality, they are feeling down in the dumps or are worried about something. You can help your partner avoid this habit and combat their anxiety by informing them that how they feel matters to them and that it is important to you that they are honest. You cannot help an anxious or depressed person feel better if you do not know how they feel.

Habit 7: Magnifying A Situation (Blowing Things Out of Proportion)

Anxious and depressed people tend to engage in something called catastrophizing. This is also called magnifying and it refers to blowing matters out of proportion in a dysfunctional way. Anxious men and women do not do this on purpose. Because they tend to over-worry or obsess about things, they can attach more importance to things that what really is there. Helping your partner drop the habit of magnifying or catastrophizing is an important step in the direction of salvaging or maintaining your relationship.

Habit 8: Not Listening

This is a habit that anxious individuals and their partners can be guilty of. Although an anxious person may hang onto your every word and *hear* you, are they really listening? Remember that anxiety-fraught individuals can misinterpret or misunderstand ambiguous words or communicated information (via text, email, et cetera). Listening, therefore, becomes a very critical skill to have in a relationship where anxiety is an issue. Drop the habit of not listening to one another and both of you will see all the ways that your relationship can be bettered.

Habit 9: Allowing Your Partner to Isolate Themselves

Depressed or anxious individuals can isolate themselves. In depressed individuals, this can be attributed to chemical signals that cause a host of symptoms that basically lead to them being more withdrawn, while in anxious persons it often may be due to avoiding situations that might trigger their worries, obsessions, or compulsions. Isolating yourself is a habit that anxious people will have to drop if they hope to get better, and as their partner, you will be making a big difference if you can help them here.

Habit 10: Managing Stress Poorly, Both Inside and Outside a Relationship

It can be argued that anxious people, by definition, have difficulty managing stress, but managing stress will is important in any relationship whether there is anxiety or not. Think about a relationship where both partners work or have busy schedules. You want to make sure that you both have time for the things that relax you or that you enjoy and also that you have ways of diffusing anger-fraught or stressful situations. Managing stress poorly can, therefore, be a bad habit in any relationship, but in relationships where one partner is anxious, this habit can result in catastrophe. Do yourself a favor and talk to your partner about how the two of you will handle situations that stress you out.

Frequently Asked Questions

1. What is anxiety?

Anxiety refers to the emotional state of being worried or afraid. As an emotion, anxiousness lies on the basic spectrum of emotions that includes happiness, sadness, disappointment and others. This emotion will be associated in some people's minds with a furrowed brow and worried facial expression; these basically representing the state of heightened awareness that essentially serves as a hallmark for anxiousness.

There is also the condition of general anxiety disorder, which takes the basic anxiety that anyone can experience and which describes a disorder characterized by a prolonged period of anxious thoughts or worries that cause dysfunction in the life of the impacted individual. Anxiety is, therefore, not dissimilar to depression in that it can characterize both a state and a disorder associated with a prolonged period in an anxious state. Although anxiousness is associated with fear, this feeling is generally regarded as an excessive state of worry, or as fear that occurs dysfunctionally, or in circumstances in which a person would not normally experience fear.

2. Are there different types of anxiety?

Psychiatrists and medical professionals have described anxiety disorders to encapsulate the different forms that worry can take. Anxiousness is associated with excessive worries or fears, but the triggers for those worries or fears can be very varied. Generalized anxiety disorder (GAD) is characterized by excessive worries about a wide variety of things or situations without a clear trigger. GAD distinct from other conditions that have a discrete trigger.

The Diagnostic and Statistical Manual defines several conditions as characterized by anxiety, although some conditions have recently been separated from the anxiety disorder moniker and have been given their own classifications. There are several conditions that are covered in this book in addition to GAD and these include social anxiety disorder (social phobia), specific phobias, obsessive-compulsive disorder (OCD), post-traumatic stress disorder, situational anxiety, and panic disorder.

3. How can anxiety impact a relationship?

Worry can have a very serious impact on a relationship. Anxious people may demonstrate excessive fear or physical symptoms that may render interacting with them difficult for people who may be unfamiliar with their condition. Anxious people also may avoid situations that can set off their disorder. This is true of people with GAD, social phobia, specific phobias, agoraphobia, post-traumatic stress disorder, and other conditions that fall under the spectrum of worry.

Although many people perceive anxiousness as being perhaps not as severely dysfunctional as other forms of mental illness (in part because anxiety is so common), anxiety remains a serious condition that can cause great dysfunction in the lives of people suffering from these conditions. Someone with obsessive-compulsive disorder, for example, may find themselves trapped in a behavior or obsessions and compulsions that renders it difficult for them to hold a job, leave the house, or have prolonged interactions with other people.

4. What causes anxiety?

The exact cause of is not clear. This is an area of active debate. It has been observed that anxiousness is more common in Western countries than in the developed world. It also has been observed that anxious symptoms are more common in females than in males. An interesting observation regarding this condition is that as groups begin to adopt external features of Westernization, anxious conditions and other forms of mental illness appear to become more common.

Of course, no one can say why anxiety happens or why it seems to impact some groups more than others. Anxiousness does appear to have a genetic component, although not all cases can be accounted for by genetics. In other words, anxiousness does tend to run in families, although some individuals may develop an anxiety disorder even though no one in their family has experienced worry. Another area of study is the role that the media plays in this condition, although this is a subject that is a long way away from reaching a conclusion.

5. Are phobias considered a type of anxiety?

Specific phobia is the name that doctors give to anxiety that is triggered by a specific object or situation. Specific phobias are interesting because they are more common than many people realize. In fact, specific phobias appear to be particularly common in Western countries like the United States, a finding that has puzzled some psychiatrists. A person with specific phobia can experience symptoms of anxiousness and panic attacks in response to being exposed to the trigger of their phobia.

An important feature of specific phobias is also that the phobic individual will experience significant worry about being exposed to their phobia and will avoid situations in which they may find themselves interacting with the object that they are afraid of. The specific phobias designation covers a wide range of phobias ranging from a fear of spiders to a fear of thunder or a fear of being naked in public. Like other anxiety disorders, phobias are associated with worries and fears that are regarded as out of proportion to the actual trigger.

6. How is anxiety treated?

As with other mental health conditions, anxiety can be treated in a number of different ways. Treatment for can generally be divided into three categories. These categories include therapy and behavior modification, medication, and alternative medicine. Anxiety disorders are unique in that although medication is an important aspect of treatment, many medication treatments for anxious conditions were not designed to treat these disorders, but others, especially depression. Indeed, antidepressant medications are among the most common treatments for anxiety. SSRIs and SNRIs (types of antidepressants) are very popular in the treatment of anxiety. As depression represents a major comorbidity that is shared with anxiousness, psychiatrists often find antidepressants almost a panacea for their patients who suffer from anxiousness as well as a depression.

7. Does anxiety have to be treated with medication?

Anxiousness does not have to be treated with medication. Indeed, unlike some other conditions that impact mental health first-line treatment for anxiety often includes modalities that do not involve medication at all. Therapy, in particular, has been shown to be effective for specific phobias.

8. Are there natural remedies for anxiety?

There are natural remedies for anxiety. These include herbal remedies, substances like inositol, and aromatherapy. Another natural, non-medication treatment for anxiousness includes transcendental meditation.

9. How common is anxiety?

Anxiety is extremely common. It is estimated that nearly one in ten people suffer from it in a given year. This number is believed to be higher in Western countries like the United States. Although many people may think of generalized anxiety disorder when they hear the word anxiety, GAD actually represents less than half of the cases of anxiety or so the psychiatric community believes. Other conditions like specific phobias, social phobia, and situational anxiety account for much of the anxiousness that is experienced worldwide.

10. How is anxiety related to depression? Why are antidepressant medications prescribed for anxiety?

Anxiety and depression can frequently co-occur. Indeed, it has been found that a large percentage of people that are diagnosed with major depressive disorder also have an anxiety disorder of some kind. Although it is not clear why these conditions tend to overlap, there is an aspect of brain chemistry dysfunction that appears to be shared between anxiety and depression.

Neurotransmitters are the molecules the brain uses to communicate across the synapses of the central nervous system (CNS). Neurotransmitters released from one end of the synapse bond to their receptor sites at the other end of the synapse, triggering a message that is carried across the neurons to their target areas. Many psychiatric medications work by modifying concentrations of neurotransmitters at the synapse, and this is true of medications that treat depression and anxiety. In particular, antidepressants commonly increase concentrations of serotonin, norepinephrine, or dopamine at the synapse, suggesting that these neurotransmitters are important in the signaling pathways related to depression and fear.

11. Is there stigma surrounding anxiety?

There is stigma surrounding many mental health conditions, including anxiety. Although one might imagine that common conditions like anxiety or depression would be associated with less stigma than others, there is still significant stigma regarding these conditions. Sometimes the stigma can take the shape of a loved one disregarding depressive or anxious symptoms because of their own subjective experiences with these conditions. Other may feel that depression and anxiety are problems that everyone faces and which can be resolved without any major intervention.

In fact, studies suggest that anxiousness persists if it is not treated. Stigma surrounding anxiety, therefore, cannot only prevent anxious people from getting the treatment they need, but it can result in incorrect information being spread regarding conditions like anxiety. Supporting anxious individuals, therefore, involves educating yourself about the condition so that you have an understanding of what it is and why it happens. Anxiety disorders can be severely debilitating and treatment is the ultimate goal.

12. Can anxiety be symptomatic of a more serious condition?

The differential diagnosis for anxiety includes a large number of conditions. This is because the brain pathway that is associated with anxiousness can be triggered by other conditions or by medications. Some conditions that are associated with anxiousness include endocrine conditions, vitamin and nutrient deficiencies, medication and substance abuse, and conditions that impact the central nervous system like multiple sclerosis. Anxiety can, therefore, be absolutely a symptom of an underlying condition rather than a primary diagnosis.

13. Are partners of anxious persons at risk for developing anxiety themselves?

There is the phenomenon of the partners of depressed people becoming depressed themselves. Although this has not been observed as frequently in anxious people, it is a development that some individuals in the mental health community warn others to be cautious about. This finding that partners of anxious people can become anxious too is perhaps related to the comorbidity that exists between anxiety and depression. In other words, the worry that develops in both partners can actually be depression that also develops an anxiety disorder component. But considering how heterogeneous anxiety disorders can be in their presentation, it cannot be said with certainty that anxiety that develops in two partners in a couple is not actually an anxious condition but depression.

14. Are there foods that can make anxiety worse?

There absolutely are foods that can make anxiousness or depression worse. Some of these include well-known foods or substances like caffeine, alcohol, and tobacco, but there are other lesser-known foods that have been shown to exacerbate anxiety symptoms. These include foods like tofu, wheat bran, canned soup, and apple juice. Recall that anxiety and depression are disorders of body chemistry, so trying to keep your body in a healthy homeostasis important. Keeping track of the things you and your partner are taking into your body is an easy way to combat worry in a relationship.

15. What is the fight or flight response and what role does it play in anxiety?

Anxiety has been shown to be related to the normal fight or flight response that is part of being a human being and responding to threats that occur in the environment. That being said, anxiety disorders are associated with the exaggerated or dysfunctional activation of the fight or flight response. Anxiousness is characterized by the activation of fight or flight at times when the stimulation of this pathway is not needed. The fight or flight response is ordinarily (and functionally) triggered by events that are perceived as threatening or harmful.

The fight or flight response is a part of the action of the sympathetic nervous system. The normal functions of the sympathetic nervous system include the regulation of the body's natural homeostasis and to trigger the fight or flight response in times of danger. The sympathetic nervous system is a part autonomic nervous system and therefore generally acts and is activated unconsciously.

The fight or flight response occurs through the work of neurotransmitters. In this case, the important neurotransmitters are epinephrine and norepinephrine, which are two important catecholamines. These are not the only neurotransmitters that play a role in the stress response as serotonin and dopamine have also been shown to be important. An important class of medications used to treat anxiety is the selective serotonin reuptake inhibitors or SSRIs, which are also used in the treatment of depression.

16. Are there conditions that can present with anxiousness but are not actually anxiety disorders?

The underlying pathway of anxiety includes disturbances in brain chemistry and activation of the sympathetic nervous system's fight or flight pathway. For this reason, there are a number of conditions that can present with anxiousness even though they are not really anxiety disorders. The differential diagnosis of conditions that present with anxiousness includes a large number of medical conditions. Although these conditions do not all cause anxiety the same way, studies suggest that the fight or flight pathway that is triggered during an anxiety symptom all represent a similar activation of certain pathways in the brain.

Underlying this mechanism is the role of specific neurotransmitters operating at the level of the synapse. The differential diagnosis for anxiety includes conditions like the following:

- Diabetes mellitus
- Endocrine disorders
- Vitamin and mineral deficiencies

- Cardiovascular disease
- Gastrointestinal disease
- Blood disorders
- Nervous system diseases including Parkinson's disease
- Medication

17. What is Body Dysmorphic Disorder and is it a type of phobia?

Some professionals group Body Dysmorphic Disorder with phobias, although it is grouped together with obsessive-compulsive disorders in the Diagnostic and Statistical Disorder. Body Dysmorphic Disorder or BDD is an obsession with a perceived body defect. It is a disorder on the anxiety spectrum and it is grouped together with OCD because individuals with this condition have a fixed notion that there is something wrong with their bodies. Body dysmorphic disorders are related to disorders like anorexia nervosa and others because these are also associated with a false perception and with anxiousness that comes along with obsessing over it.

Researchers have noted that body dysmorphic disorder is common in men as well as women, and it may be becoming more common over time. This is an interesting area of study because it suggests that anxiety (although associated with a clear pathway in the brain) can be initiated or reinforced by triggers within the environment. For example, a form of body dysmorphic disorder that is common in men is the so-called bigorexia. Bigorexia is the colloquial term for men who are obsessed with their muscular development and who became anxious and obsessed with their belief that they are "not big enough." An essential component of body dysmorphic disorder is the element of unreality that is associated with it.

In other words, individuals with body dysmorphic disorder (including so-called bigorexia) have perceptions about their body that are unrealistic or purely false. For example, a very muscular individual may be obsessed with the notion that they are "skinny" or "small" and in consequence, need to spend more time in the gym. Further studies in this area may reveal the connection the social factors (including television and other media) have in the development of anxiety disorders.

Conclusion

Anxiousness does not have to derail your life or the life of your partner. If you are in a relationship where anxiety is an issue, you should take comfort in knowing that anxious symptoms can be managed effectively in various ways, relieving the hold that anxious thoughts have on your relationship. One of the goals of this book has been to teach the reader what worry is so that they can recognize it. Part of what makes anxiousness so difficult to manage in relationships is that many people do not have an accurate understanding of what anxiety is rendering the simple act of recognizing it a difficult one.

As the reader has learned in this book, anxiousness impacts millions of people worldwide at any given time, with some estimating that as many ten percent of the population will experience an anxiety symptom in a given year. Anxiety can be defined as an emotion characterized by excessive worries or fears. It is this anxious emotion that allows a class of disorders referred to as anxiety disorders to be described. These disorders are all characterized by the experience of anxiousness, although how the feeling manifests may differ from one condition to the next.

Perhaps the most well-known anxiety disorder is what psychologists refer to as generalized anxiety disorder. This is the disorder that some people are referring to when they talk about anxiety, although it is estimated to account for slightly less than fifty percent of all cases of anxiousness. A common category of disorders characterized by anxiety is the specific phobias. Specific phobias are associated with excessive fear around a specific object or trigger, like crowds, spiders, or speaking publicly.

The first step to successfully dealing with anxiousness in the relationship setting is to educate yourself enough on the subject so that you can understand the condition and all the ways that it may surface in a relationship. The goal of the first chapter was to give you a thorough understanding of what anxiety is and why anxiety may be more common in certain parts of the world and certain groups. This allows you not only to approach the anxiety in your relationship from the standpoint of knowledge, but it also permits you to show sympathy for your partner's anxiety because you understand it better and have an idea of where it may be coming from.

Being fully educated about worry requires that you have a basic understanding of anxiety disorders. Although many relationships may be characterized by the general anxiety that is associated with generalized anxiety disorder, other conditions like panic disorder, specific phobias, obsessive-compulsive disorder, or post-traumatic stress disorder have unique symptoms which makes dealing with them a unique ordeal. The goal is not necessarily that the reader should know how each disorder should be managed, but at least to be able to recognize what type of anxiety their partner suffers from and to be aware that different types of anxiousness should be managed differently.

The question of where anxiety comes from is a loaded one. Although it has been observed that this condition does frequently run in families, it has also been found that anxiety appears to be more common in Western countries than developing countries (in addition to other notable demographic trends). A potentially important cause of anxiety is the dysfunctional relationships that some men and women may experience in their youth. This is the idea behind attachment theory: the model that shows how children learn how to interact with other people and their environment based on the relationship they have with their primary caregiver. As this is a book focusing on relationships, understanding the role that attachment plays as a possible cause of later anxiety can allow the sympathy that a partner shows for their significant other to become true empathy: another goal of this book.

Anxiety can be treated successfully, providing relief for the millions of men and women in relationships and out of them that deal with anxiousness. Anxious symptoms can be treated with medication, but it can also be treated successfully with therapy, dietary changes, and natural remedies. These natural remedies include things like herbs found in the environment, inositol, and transcendental meditation. Although more research has to be done to show how effective these treatments are, they represent another option for people looking for alternatives to the more common medication and therapeutic options.

This would not be an effective book about dealing with anxiousness in relationships if it did not provide the reader with tips they can follow to help them maintain their relationship in the face of worry. It is not easy dealing with anxiousness either as the individual suffering from it or as the partner of the anxious individual, and this is a concept that this book recognizes. Therefore, the last two chapters of the book focused on providing the reader with tips they can use to support their partner through their anxiety, or to keep them from making their partner's anxiety worse.

An important fact to know about anxiety is that it usually does not go away on its own. If anxiety is left untreated, it will persist, potentially derailing the anxious individual's familial and romantic relationships and preventing them from forming new, enduring ones. The goal of this book is to help the partner of the anxious person become more supportive, which may be so important for that person that it can change the course of their life. Anxiety can be beaten, but it will take effort and reading this book was the first step in your accomplishment of this important work.

Made in the USA
Monee, IL
30 April 2020